Yes You Can Retire

A simple guide to retirement success

By Craig Richard Burton

ISBN: 9798527964677

Unless designate otherwise all Scripture quoted is from the New International Version (NIV) 1984
Zondervan

Printed in Grand Rapids, Michigan
First Edition
2 3 4 5 6 7

Editors: Diane Collett and Laurie Mains

Table of Contents

ACKNOWLEDGMENTS

Thanks to family members who encouraged me in the process of writing this book, David & Karen Mains, Valerie & Steve Bell. Thanks to Diane Collett and Laurie Mains for the editing skills and helpful suggestions.

Preface

So, I know what you're thinking. Why do we need another book on financial management and retirement planning? Well, here's my take on the subject: A lot of workers today don't feel they can retire either because they don't feel like they have enough money or they don't know how to navigate the planning process. Some feel that their financial situations are so bad that they will have to keep working for the rest of their lives. This book tells you that you can have a successful retirement if you are willing to follow some simple guidelines. They are not always easy but they are understandable and they are doable if you are willing to discipline yourself to follow them. After reading the book you will know that you can retire and that you can do it successfully.

Much of the financial information we have today is put out by "financial experts," people who have degrees and are licensed investors. Some of the big names in the field are multi-millionaires who have made fortunes off of their books and TV programs. Some of these pros just can't relate to the majority of us "the little guys" like you and me. It is kind of like professional sports. We love our favorite teams and we think we can identify with our sports heroes, until we read about the outrageous salaries they make. We hear of a player leaving his team because is only making $25 million. So he goes to another team that offers him $75 million. Suddenly we realize these people are not like us. They are in a different world and they don't relate to ordinary folks like you and me. Others in the finance field are young and experienced. I have read articles by 30-year-olds telling you and me how to plan for retirement. It reminds me what someone said about life coaches. "Why is every life coach I know 24 years old and still living in his or her parents' basement?"

This book is different. It is written by an ordinary person who has had a family, a mortgage, and who has never made much money. However, I have managed my money well and as I've entered into retirement I find myself financially "sitting pretty." I have done it through living simply and through having a disciplined and consistent approach to handling money. If you want to learn how to do the same, this book is for you. If you want to learn how to get rich, read another book. But if you want to learn how to handle money successfully in a smart and simple way from someone who is not a billionaire but from one of the "little guys," probably like you, read on.

Introduction

Some time ago I had a long phone conversation with a financial advisor. In the midst of our conversation he told me, "You are in better financial shape than anyone I have dealt with in two or three years." I thought to myself, how can this possibly be? I have made a small salary all of my life and I don't have nearly the amount of money socked away that "financial experts" say a person needs in order to retire. My wife and I lead a very modest financial lifestyle. How can I possibly be better off than anyone the financial advisor has spoken to in the past two or three years? Now, considering the fact that this man's job mostly involves speaking with people about their retirement situations, his statement is quite remarkable.

At the same time as I am writing this, our nation and world is in the midst of a catastrophic pandemic. We are also on the precipice of a great financial collapse. As I drive through my community I have seen long lines of cars at food centers because people have lost their jobs. Now people getting help at these food centers are by-in-large not homeless or street people. They are people who have had good jobs and who live in nice homes but they don't have money to pay for their groceries. This scenario is being played out all over the country and I imagine all over the world. Yet my situation is different. I have just recently retired and although the markets have tanked, I feel somewhat secure financially and I am not worried about how I'm going to make my mortgage payment or put food on the table. My conversation with the financial advisor had to do with whether or not I should put hundreds of thousands of cash into stocks or mutual funds due to the recent drop in the markets. My guess is that not a lot of people today are in the financial position to even begin to consider such a thing. CNN Money reports that 40% of Americans can't afford a $400 emergency. Most Americans have little to nothing saved for retirement. A 2018 study by Northwestern Mutual, claims that one-third of Baby Boomers have less than $25,000 put away for their golden years. So let me say this: I am not a financial expert by any means. I don't have a degree in finance and I am not licensed as a financial advisor. Neither am I wealthy by any stretch of the imagination. I live a simple lifestyle and within my means but I don't have any financial worries. I have just retired and I live in a brand new house that is completely paid off. Three years ago when I bought my new car, I paid cash for it. When the financial markets dropped dramatically it didn't faze me one bit because I have a secure monetary plan that is not dependent on how the Dow Jones or S&P 500 markets perform. If you would like to know how I got where I am, keep reading. I believe this book can also help you to become financially secure when you reach retirement. The title of this book pretty well explains what it's about:

"Yes You Can Retire" a simple guide for retirement success.
Many don't think that they can retire because they don't make enough money. But that is not the case. Even small the small wage earner who I call "the little guy" can have a good retirement by planning properly. So don't say you will never be able to do it. Yes you can retire if you follow the simple steps in this book. I did it and so can you.

I also need to tell you that I am a Christian, a recently retired minister. Much of what I know and have learned over the years has come from this perspective. I will use principles from the Bible when appropriate to illustrate important financial truths. Wisdom is the key to handling money. Wisdom by my definition is, "The ability to look at life and life's challenges from God's point of view." Proverbs 4:17 reads, "Wisdom is supreme; therefore get wisdom. Though it cost all you have, get understanding." I have noticed over the years that some books on finances, even though written by Christians, say very little about the Bible. This book, however, is written from a Biblical perspective. So for these two reasons I feel the book is unique. It is written to the little guy from a little guy and it is integrated with scriptural principles.

Chapter 1

Change the Way You Think about Money

Maybe you are head over your heels in debt and you are paying high interest on your credit cards. Maybe you are mortgaged to the hilt and the financial crisis has got you wondering if you're going to lose your home. Perhaps you are a person that lives paycheck to paycheck or maybe you are one of the ones who can't handle a $400 financial emergency. Maybe you are someone who would like to retire but feel like you are going to have to work for the rest of your life because you have very little retirement savings. A lot of us as Americans are in this category. Please understand it is not a matter of making more money. A lot of people think that the answer to their financial woes is to make more money. Making more money usually means spending more which for many means more debt and more financial difficulties. I have and you probably have also known individuals who have made tons of money yet who can hardly pay their bills and are drowning in debt. The answer for many who have financial problems is not to make more money but it is to change the way they think about money. This includes thinking differently about not only spending but the way we save money and even how we view the purpose of money. If you are willing to change the way you think about money, you can have a secure and worry free financial future. It will take time. There are no easy quick fixes, but it will happen if you apply the principles in this book. But if you want to keep doing what you're doing and are expecting a miracle in your finances, you are on the road to disaster. Remember, one definition of insanity is doing the same thing over and over and expecting a different result. This is the thinking of the alcoholic and the drug addict and often the person who cannot handle money. Your circumstances will not change until your thinking does. If you have financial problems you need to think about money and the way you handle it in a different way. For some people their financial problems will never go away because of the way they think. They are always dreaming, "If I only made more money." What they need to be thinking, however, is, "How I can learn to handle my money wisely?"

For some people their financial problems will never go away because of the way they think. They are always dreaming, "If I only made more money." What they need to be thinking, however, is, "How I can learn to handle my money wisely?"

Chapter 2

The Goal: Learn to Live Well, Within Your Means

The financial goal of most people is to become rich. In a recent year the North American Association of State and Provincial Lotteries claimed that Americans have spent 70.15 billion dollars on lottery tickets. One estimate is that 90 million Americans play the lottery every year. Why are so many people purchasing lottery tickets? Is it so they can meet their monthly bills, make their car payments, and put groceries on the table? No, you don't have to win the lottery to do all this. People play the lottery because they want to get rich.

A national survey showed to what extent people would go in order to gain 10 million dollars. Twenty-five percent would abandon their family, 25 percent would abandon their church, 23 percent would become a prostitute for a week, 16 percent would give up their American citizenship, 16 percent would leave their spouse, and 3 percent would put their children up for adoption. Seven percent said they would murder for the money, 6 percent would change their race, and 4 percent would change their sex (Patterson, James & Kim, Peter, *The Day America Told the Truth: What People Really Believe About Everything That Really Matters.* New York, Prentice Hall, 1991).

What the Bible says about the desire to get wealthy may shock you. "A faithful person will be richly blessed, but one eager to get rich will not go unpunished" (Proverbs 28:20).

First Timothy 6:9–10 says, "Those who want to get rich fall into temptation and a trap and into many foolish and harmful desires that plunge people into ruin and destruction. For the love of money is a root of all kinds of evil. Some people, eager for money, have wandered from the faith and pierced themselves with many griefs."

People who want to get rich are tempted to purchase homes and cars they can't afford. They make risky investments and some even do illegal things that land them in prison. Notice, however, the Bible doesn't say that "money is a root of all evil," but rather that "the love of money is a root of all kinds of evil." See the difference? Some falsely accuse the Bible of teaching that money is evil. It is not true. Money can be used for many good things, such as providing for the needs of our families, helping the poor, building hospitals, and more. So on one hand we appreciate how money can provide many good things, including serving the purposes of God, but on the other hand we realize its danger. When we love money or when we desire to become rich, wealth suddenly becomes our god and we end up doing a lot of destructive and dumb things. Take, for example, the man who works day and night in order to obtain the "good life" but neglects his family in the process. His kids end up with emotional problems because they felt their dad never loved them and rarely had time for them. What their dad did wasn't illegal, but his love of money took him away from his kids when they needed him.

A woman refuses to report her husband's death to Social Security. She continues to collect his benefits for several years until she is finally caught and faces fines and prison. In both cases the love of money and or the misuse of it led to destruction.

I'm saying, there are a lot of ways the love of money can raise its ugly head. Often we don't realize that we have the disease but it will, according to the Bible, reap all kinds of destruction in our lives. If your desire is to get rich I can't help you, because this book is not about getting rich; it is about learning to thrive within your means. If you desire to get rich, you'll never be happy because you will never be satisfied. I've met just a few wealthy people who are truly happy. On the other hand, I've met a lot of people with modest incomes who seem very happy. Go figure! More importantly, if you want to get rich you'll probably do something stupid that will make your financial situation worse than it already is. So get the idea out of your head that you want to be wealthy. Instead, make it your goal to live well, within your means. Learn to be content with this.

The Bible says a lot about money. Did you know that most of the parables (stories) of Jesus had something to do with money or material possessions? One of these parables is found in Matthew 25. It is known as the Parable of the Talents.

> "Again, it will be like a man going on a journey, who called his servants and entrusted his wealth to them. To one he gave five bags of gold, to another two bags, and to another one bag, each according to his ability. Then he went on his journey. The man who had received the five bags of god went at once and put his money to work and gained five more. So also, the one with two bags of gold gained two more. But the man who had received one bag of gold went off, dug a hole in the ground and hid his master's money.
>
> "After a long time the master of those servants returned and settled accounts with them. The man who had received five bags of gold brought the other five. 'Master,' he said, 'you entrusted me with five bags of gold. See, I have gained five more.'
>
> "His master replied, 'Well done, good and faithful servant! You have been faithful with a few things; I will put you in charge of many things. Come and share your master's happiness!'
>
> "The man with the two bags of gold also came. 'Master,' he said, 'you entrusted me with two bags of gold; see, I have gained two more.'
>
> "His master replied, 'Well done, good and

faithful servant! You have been faithful with a few things; I will put you in charge of many things. Come and share your master's happiness!'

"Then the man who had received one bag of gold came. 'Master,' he said, 'I knew that you are a hard man, harvesting where you have not sown and gathering where you have not scattered seed. So, I was afraid and went out and hid your gold in the ground. See, here is what belongs to you.'

"His master replied, 'You wicked, lazy servant! So you knew that I harvest where I have not sown and gather where I have not scattered seed? Well then, you should have put my money on deposit with the bankers, so that when I returned I would have received it back with interest.

"'So take the bag of gold from him and give it to the one who has ten bags. For whoever has will be given more, and they will have an abundance. Whoever does not have, even what they have will be taken from him. And throw that worthless servant outside, into the darkness, where there will be weeping and gnashing of teeth'" (14–30).

If we think of the parable in more current terms, it might sound like this: A businessman went on a long business trip. Before he left, he gave three of his employees differing amounts of money. To one he gave 50 thousand dollars. To another he gave 20 thousand and to the third he gave 10 thousand. When he came back, he called his employees to see what they had done with the money he had told them to invest. The first and second employees both had doubled their money but the last individual hid his money in his mattress because he was afraid. His boss ridiculed him: "Couldn't you at least have invested my money in the bank? Did you have to hide it in your bedroom and get absolutely no return?"

Here's the lesson from the parable: Everything we have, our money, homes, cars, belongs to God. We are not owners; rather, we are stewards of his possessions. While he has entrusted them to our care, we are to manage them to the best of our abilities. This means we take care of our property and faithfully watch over our finances. Our goal is not to become rich but to be good stewards of what he has given us to manage. It is to learn to live within our means so that when we want to stop working we will be able to have a comfortable retirement.

In another passage, 1 Timothy 6:6, the writer says that we should be content with what we have. "But godliness with contentment is great gain." That means we should strive not to be rich but to be happy and thankful for what we have. We are not constantly pushing for newer, nicer, and better, nor are we trying to keep up with the Joneses. We are content with what we have.

The implication is that we learn to live within our means. If we make $100,000 a year we shouldn't spend $150,000 a year. If we make $50,000 we shouldn't spend $70,000. We might think this is obvious, and it is. But one study suggests that 46 percent of Americans spend more than they make. It may be obvious, but many aren't getting it. (NGPF, Next Gen Personal Finance, February 26, 2018)

So here is a financial goal that I have lived by for years: "Being a steward of God's money, I will endeavor to live well, within my means." Notice where the comma is. I want to live well, meaning to enjoy the good things God has given to me, but I want to do it within my income. It also means to live well, spending less than what I make. My goal is not to spend exactly what I make, because I want to have extra, so I can do other things like have a retirement fund and an emergency fund, give to the needy, and so on. But we'll talk about those things later. For now, let's just concentrate on this one simple goal, which almost half of Americans don't do, and that is to live well, within our means. It is not to get rich or to live on the edge financially but to live contentedly within what we make. If you can burn this ambition within you with great resolve, I can show you how to get your financial house in order and start enjoying your retirement instead of worrying about running out of money. Where do we start?

Chapter 3

Get Out of Debt

Having debt is not a good thing. The Bible says the borrower is servant to the lender, and that is true (Proverbs 22:7). People to whom we owe money own us, so to speak. Just see what happens when you miss a few car payments. The guys at Friendly Sam's Used Cars suddenly aren't so friendly. If we continue to miss payments, they'll take back what we thought was ours. I have never had debt except to purchase a house. I never bought a car on payments, nor have I ever owed interest on a credit card. I went to college and seminary without a student loan and in fact I also paid for my wife's last two years of college without taking out a loan. I realize that is very hard to do today, but you get my point. It is a wonderful, freeing thing to owe no one anything. In fact, the Bible says the only debt we should have is the debt to love one another (Romans 13:8). You will feel much better when you have no debts and you will be able to live on a lot less also.

So let's start by making a list of all the people you owe money to: credit cards, school loans, car payments, and how much you owe to each. Here is what you are going to do: You will go after these debts with a vengeance. Start paying off the smallest ones first so you feel like you are making progress, then go to the next biggest, and then the next. In order to do this you may have to get a part-time job, cut the cable, quit going out to eat for a while, stop taking vacations until it happens. You will hurt and sacrifice, but when you pay everything off, you will feel like a new man or woman. Paying off debt is like the sacrifice you made when you went to college. It took all your time and your money. But when you finished most likely you were able to get a much better paying job while doing something you really wanted to do.* This is how it was for me and it worked, but it took great sacrifice. Paying off those debts may be the hardest thing you ever do, but it will be well worth it. My parents went through the Great Depression and they never bought things on credit. The idea was, if you didn't have the money you didn't buy it. This is the principle I have lived by all my life, and I have never regretted it.

*(Many studies suggest that college grads on average make more than those who do not have bachelor's degrees. For example CNN Business June 6, 2019 quotes a study by the Federal Reserve Bank of New York. The study suggests that the average salary for college grads is $78,000 compared to the $45,000 average salary made by the worker who has only a high school education)

The idea was, if you didn't have the money for it, you didn't buy it. This is the principle I have lived by all my life, and I have never regretted it.

Other people had nicer cars but mine was paid for and I never lost sleep at night worrying about the debt on my credit cards. I like the old bumper sticker that read, "Don't laugh at this car; it's paid for." So listen up. While you are paying off those credit cards you will no longer purchase things on credit. Your new rule is, you pay cash for everything. There is no use killing yourself to pay your credit cards if you are continuing to make charges. This is like biting off your nose to spite your face. Pay cash or make purchases from a debit card only from now on. If you need to cut up your credit cards because they're too tempting for you, go for it.

Chapter 4

Track your Spending

A lot of people have no idea how much they spend over a month or a year. So from now on write down how much you spend and what you spend it for. An easy way to do this is by simply saving your receipts. Track your spending for at least a month, preferably two, or even a year. A friend told me that he could never do this. He doesn't like to keep records, and doing so would "drive him nuts". Well, it is not hard at all. Just save the receipts and record the amounts into your ledger or spreadsheet. This should also include your cash expenditures. Then you will know exactly where your money goes and you will know what adjustments to make. I have been tracking my spending for over thirty years, and I can tell you how much I spend on medical and how much I spend on groceries and housing, everything. I've got it all down on my computer. And here's the deal: You can make better financial decisions if you know where your money goes. Imagine a business having no idea how much they spent on advertising or on building maintenance or on salaries. They would have no idea if they could hire a new employee or if they could expand their product line. Tracking your spending will help you to make a budget which is absolutely imperative if you want to take charge of your finances.

Chapter 5

Make a Budget

After you track your spending, you can make a budget for every category of your costs. So, for example, you make $75,000 a year. You will have to cut up your financial pie to not exceed this total. "Let's see, last year we spent $5,000 on medical, so we'll budget about the same for this next year. We spent $12,000 on housing, and we can't really change that at this point. But look at this: We spent $10,000 on eating out and entertainment. I think in order to live within our $75,000 salary we are going to have to cut that to $5000 a year. Then we can make all the other categories work as well."

You get the picture. You track your spending and you fit everything into your salary pie, however much you need to spend on each category. When you see you are over your salary, you cut categories until they all fit into the total. Creating a budget takes some work, but it is necessary in order to live well, within your means, which, as you remember, is your goal. There are some good online tools for creating budgets. I happen to use Quicken but there may be some other programs that better fit your needs. Mint and Personal Capital are popular programs today. The nice thing about a computer program is that it figures your totals and reports automatically. After you have entered your expenditures, you just click on your budget report and it shows you exactly where you stand. It shows you in which areas you have gone over budget and where you have a surplus. You can easily see your monthly income versus expenses so you know exactly where you are. It also simplifies things during taxes. You'll have all your information for your accountant with a push of a button. I have self prepared my taxes for years with a tax software program. Having up-to-date financial records on my computer program makes it fun and easy to do so. I never dread tax time as a lot of people do because they feel it is drudgery to go through all their records to get them ready for the accountant. If you track all of your spending & earnings on your computer all you have to do is print out your reports and you're ready to go.

Some people think that having a budget is boring and restrictive. I will agree that it might be a little boring but it is far from restrictive. To the contrary, having a budget is freeing because you know whether you can afford to buy something or not. It will fit into the budget or it will not.

For example, you will know if you can afford to purchase that new refrigerator or hire the house cleaner as opposed to continuing to dust and vacuum yourself. All you have to do is look at your budget and it will give you your answer. "Sorry, we've already used up our budget for that this month." So you live with those sad facts. You stay home and eat frozen pizza, or restrict yourself to shopping the 70 percent off rack at Wal-Mart. But here's the good part: When there is money in the budget to do something or buy something, you can do it and really enjoy it without having to worry about not being able to afford it. "I know we can afford this vacation, because we've budgeted for it." This happened to me regarding my recent retirement. Even though I was of retirement age I felt guilty for even considering retiring. Friends and family members my age and older keep working and I thought maybe I should, too. I thought if they couldn't afford to retire maybe I couldn't either. But I had the numbers and knew exactly how much I would need to make, and I knew exactly what my retirement income would be. So the smart thing to do for me was to retire and enjoy it.

But here's the good part: When there is money in the budget to do something or buy something, you can do it and really enjoy it without having to worry about not being able to afford it.

Now, while I am on the subject of retirement, let me say this: If you are retired, you absolutely need to have a budget. You need to know how much you should draw from your IRA and 401(k) to cover your expenses. If you don't estimate correctly, you can run out of money in your retirement years, and this is something none of us wants to do.

The last thing I want to say about budgets is that you need to regularly review them. You don't set it up once and forget about it. You have to adjust it as you go along because your expenses can change over time. For example, your medical expenses may be more this year than last, so you will have to adjust your allotments. If you project that your expenses will be higher in one area, you should adjust some other category downward to compensate. Remember, it's all like a pie. If you spend more in medical, you will have to spend less in another category like entertainment. You will need to periodically review your budget. I review mine monthly, and I pay special attention to the quarterly budget reports. (If you track your finances through a software program, budget reports are simple to run.) Then I can project pretty well how I will probably do for the entire year. This is the goal, to have all your expense categories under your total income for the year. Budgets are great tools only if you live by them. It makes no sense to make a budget and not live within your financial limits. If you can discipline yourself to set it up and live within it, it will free you not only financially but emotionally. Imagine being able to buy a new car using cash, with no worries about affording it because you have saved and budgeted for it. I'll never forget the look on the car dealer's face when he asked me how I was going to finance the new car I had just purchased. When I said, "I'll pay cash," he looked like he was in a state of shock! Perhaps he'd never seen it done before. But you can do it too if you learn to live within your means, live within a workable budget, and save.

Chapter 6

Build Up your Savings

According to *GoBankingRates.com* 32 percent of Americans have no savings and 58 percent of Americans have saved less than $1,000. At the same time, the Survey of Consumer Finances by the U.S. Federal Reserve estimates that the mean amount of credit card debt per American is $5,700. (Every month the Federal Reserve releases debt statistics. Do an internet search for "Average Credit Card Debt, Federal Reserve)_So it sounds like a lot of us are losing ground. Why is it important to have a savings account? Cash is king, as some people say, especially when there is a financial crisis like there has been lately where people are losing their jobs and can't buy groceries or pay their rent. When such a crisis comes, you won't have to stand in bread lines* and they won't turn off your electricity, since you've secured a healthy savings. Financial advisors say that you should aim for having three to six months' salary stashed away in savings in case you ever become unemployed. But I would say, shoot for a year to two years. It might take that long to get back on your feet. A healthy savings also gives you buying power. Usually you can get a better deal on a car if you make a cash offer. Years ago I paid cash for a van that had only 8,000 miles on it. It was cash that I had earned off the interest on my savings back in the day when savings accounts paid great interest. I got such a good deal that when I turned around and sold it a year or two later, I had only lost about five hundred dollars after putting 20 thousand more miles on the vehicle.

*Bread lines were common during the Great Depression, but returned during the Covid 19 pandemic as thousands were suddenly out of work and some had to receive assistance through government and private food banks.

A lot of people think they don't make enough money to save. But in many cases if they could get rid of the debt on their credit cards and their car payments and other loans, they would be able to do it fairly easily. Savings is something that should be put right into the budget. A good rule of thumb is to put 10 percent of your money into savings every paycheck. The way to do it is to have it taken right out of your paycheck. Have your employer, if you have direct deposit, send it right to your savings account. That way you will never even miss it. You can also use the internet to find higher-interest savings accounts than what your local bank offers. Or you can check out credit unions. Both of these options are federally insured up to certain amounts, which is very reassuring.

Doing the right thing over a long period of time pays great dividends. Going to the gym once and working out doesn't do too much. But if a person goes every day for two years and works out, he or she can lose weight, gain muscle mass, and get into great cardiovascular shape. The same is true for savings. If a person can save for example a thousand dollars a month, he/she can have a great savings in 10 years, especially with compound interest. For example if you saved $1000 a month at three percent interest for 10 years, you would have a total of $141,090. If you did the same thing for 20 years you would have a savings of $330,122. How would you like to have that much money in your savings account? On the other hand, if you have to buy things on credit, the lender gets the great financial advantage. For example, if you take out a $165,000 mortgage over 30 years at a 4.5 percent interest rate, over the life of the loan you will pay $135,971 just in interest. I'm not suggesting that you should be able to purchase a home with cash, because most people can't. I'm only demonstrating that it is a lot better to have interest working for you than against you. Remember, cash is king. It protects you in times of crisis, it gives you better buying power, and it grows incredibly through the miracle of compounding.

Financial Hero Number 1

There are three people who have influenced the way I deal with money. By far the most influential was my father, Wilfred L. Burton. I would put my mother in the same influential category but my father ruled the roost, and he determined the way money was to be handled in our home.

My parents were born in the early part of the twentieth century, and they faced incredible times of financial hardship, as did most people who lived in America back then.

W.L. Burton, College Music Professor

First they lived through World War I, and then they faced the flu of 1918 (known as the Spanish Flu), from which an estimated 675,000 Americans perished. Then they faced the Great Depression of the 1930s (they were married in 1939), and finally World War II. Their generation knew suffering that most people my age could not imagine. All of this made a profound impact upon the way my parents thought about and handled money. In the early 1930s, right at the height of the Great Depression, my dad was a college student in Chicago. He told me that he and his college roommate used to go to a restaurant and order a bowl of soup between them. They would also order a bottle of ketchup, which they would empty into their soup just to have something of substance in their stomachs. After they'd done this a few times, the restaurant owner got wise to them and put an end to it. I have never known such hunger or the kind of poverty the people of that generation knew. My father was one of thousands of Americans who lost their life savings when many of the banks went belly up. These experiences shaped the way my parents lived and the way they raised me. Both worked extremely hard because they never forgot the financial struggles of those lean years. Back in the fifties and sixties, my mother was one of the few mothers I knew who worked outside the home. Today two-income households are the norm, but that wasn't the case when I grew up. The reason is, my parents had an underlying fear of being poor again like they were in the Great Depression. So they rarely went out to eat. Vacations were only to visit my grandparents in Des Moines, Iowa. There were no cruises or trips to Disney World. Most everything we had was purchased second hand. In our basement were several broken-down washing machines that my father would use for parts when our main unit went kaput. Above all, my parents saved like money was going out of style. When I was about 10 years old, my mother made the mistake of telling me that she and my dad had accumulated the huge amount of $12,000 in their savings. Nobody had $12,000 in their savings at that time; it was enough to buy a Cadillac or two, maybe three. Not my dad, however. He drove old clunkers that he had paid cash for. I was a bit envious of friends whose parents drove new cars. When I was in high school we had a couple of rusty, ugly old vehicles, and they would often break down or get flat tires. I remember in a single week running out of gas twice in one of my dad's cars because the gas gage didn't work. During the same week, the car had a flat tire. My dad didn't believe in buying new tires or even newer tires.

Then there was the stuff my parents collected (all second hand), which filled the house. They just couldn't throw things away. Well, this was the financial situation in the home in which I was raised. My father expected me to work hard and to save money and never ever purchase something on credit. We weren't poor and we weren't hungry, but there was not a thought of purchasing some expensive toy like my friends had. When money went into the savings, it didn't come out unless there was a really great reason, which there never was as far as I remember.

Craig as a teenager with his parents

When money went into the savings, it didn't come out unless there was a really great reason, which there never was as far as I remember.

When I was young, my father had me open a savings account, which I periodically made deposits into. I never withdrew from it until I was in college. Then I purchased a small, cheap stereo that cost me $39, and I felt really guilty about it. That was considered an "unnecessary purchase". Instead that money could have been accumulating interest.

My parents both died at the age of 69.They worked very hard, and my father was paid peanuts at his job at which he worked terribly long hours. He would leave every morning before I woke up to take the train to Chicago, and he would return after I was asleep each night. I don't remember an evening meal that he shared with us. This is just the way it was, but at the end of his life he had accumulated quite a bit. He had a beautiful home in a nice Chicago suburb, an 80-acre farm which he purchased in 1962 for $600 an acre, another home near the farm, which he rented out, and a trailer in a retirement community in Florida. The most he ever made from his job was $17,000 a year, and that was in the very later part of his working years. For most of his career, he made much less. I remember looking at his check stub when I was in high school. It was $600 for the entire month.

So here was the greatest influence on my financial philosophy. I learned from my dad to live within my means, to never purchase on credit, to not buy frivolous toys, and above all, to save. My father never invested in the stock market or mutual funds. He just put a lot of what he made into banks. Not just one bank, mind you. When I became the executor of my parent's estate, I found quite a few banks with differing amounts, some of which were somewhat small. This is because of what happened to my dad after the stock market collapsed in 1929. He never forgot about losing his life savings after many banks went under and closed. I remember him telling me, "Don't put your eggs in one basket."

I learned from my dad to live within my means, to never purchase on credit, to not buy frivolous toys, and above all, to save.

Sometimes my father would speak to me about how to handle money, but mostly he taught me by his example. This is, I believe, the major way we communicate our values to our children.

I have two older sisters who do not share my parents' financial philosophy. Sometimes I look at them and think, "*Didn't we have the same father"?* Well, this is what happens when we marry someone. Rarely do our spouses have the same spending habits and value on money, so we adapt to their way of doing things or they adapt to us, or we compromise.

This was true in my situation. I married my high school sweetheart, who lived less than a mile from where I grew up. Although our parents had similar values and religious views, their spending patterns were quite different. Mary's parents were conservative but were a lot freer in their spending habits. They often drove new cars, went out to eat, and by and large they were not savers. So coming from different backgrounds, we clashed in our spending practices and overall financial philosophies. As Dave Ramsey, the well-known financial author and radio host suggests, "In every marriage there is a nerd and a free spirit." The nerd is thrifty and keeps records, saves money, and so on. The free spirit wants to spend and isn't concerned about budgets and savings accounts. You can guess who was who in our situation. We did clash but eventually came to the meeting of minds. Mary learned the importance of becoming more frugal and I learned to loosen the financial strings. I bought our first new car for one reason only, to show Mary that I was not the tightwad I suspected she thought I was. I even took our family to Disney World, something my father never would have done. I learned to go out to eat and to go on fun family vacations but at the same time always keeping my father's financial principles intact. We both changed for the better. As a pastor I would tell the newlyweds I counseled that our differences in marriage are like a hammer. We can use them as a tool or a weapon. If we use them as a tool, we can build something really unique and beautiful. It is up to each couple to decide which they are going to do.

Chapter 7

Give Some Away

You might not think giving money away is an important part of financial management, but it is just as important as saving. Let me repeat, in case you missed it: Giving is just as important in terms of properly handling our money as is saving. Within each of us God has created the need to give, and when we neglect it, we become inwardly focused, self consuming, and miserable. When God commanded us to give, it wasn't because he needed our money. He wasn't worried about going bankrupt if we don't put our money in the offering plate or don't make our online contribution. He owns everything already or, as the Bible says, he owns the cattle on a thousand hills (Psalm 50:10). God commanded us to give because we desperately need to do so. Others are, of course, blessed by our giving; but we also need to give for our own emotional well-being.

When I was in high school, the pastor at my church told the story of a minister who was called to conduct the funeral of a wealthy man he did not know. When he got to the funeral home, he was surprised to find that there was only one person who had shown up for the service, the widow of the wealthy man. The pastor didn't know what he should do. Should he not preach the entire message that he thought would be given to a larger audience? The man's widow, however, encouraged the minister to proceed as usual. So he did. Afterwards the minister asked the woman, "Why is it that not one single person came to your husband's funeral?" She replied, "Rev., my husband never gave anything to anyone."

I met such an old miser in rural Minnesota where I was the pastor of a country church. He was an 82-year-old farmer who lived by himself. He was totally alone, had no children, and had never been married. As far as I knew, he didn't have any friends. But the word was that he was worth millions. He owned all sorts of farms. I was shocked to see his house was in disrepair and that he drove an old rusty pickup truck. People who can't give are often afraid to spend money even on themselves. So, I visited the old farmer one afternoon and introduced myself as the minister at the church a couple of miles down the road. As we talked on his front porch in a couple of rusty old chairs, I could tell he was not a churchgoer and was very uncomfortable speaking with a preacher. I basically did the talking because he didn't seem to be in the mood for conversation. To everything I said, he replied, What? Huh?" The man was obviously hard of hearing, or so I thought. Finally, I asked him if he would like to visit our church the next Sunday. He immediately replied with a loud, "No!" The man could hear everything I had said. He just didn't like what he was hearing. In any case, he certainly didn't seem very happy. From what I could tell, his stinginess had isolated him from others and had imprisoned him in his own private world.

Financial Hero Number 2

I told you I have three financial heroes that I want to share with you. The first was my own father whom I admired because of what he taught me about saving and frugality. The second set of heroes was my wife's parents, Stan and Gaile Benson. Although they had also lived during the Depression years, they as I already mentioned, were a lot less frugal than my parents. What made them financial heroes to me was their incredible generosity. While my father was a saver, he was not a giver. I remember my mother handing me a dollar as I was on my way to church. "Here" she whispered, "Put this in the offering plate and don't tell your

Stan & Gaile Benson on Mary's graduation from college

father." Mary's parents were just the opposite of mine. When I was dating her, I would see piles of clothes in the living room and often extra furniture sticking out where it seemed to not belong. What are these clothes for?" I would ask. "Oh, that's for the Johnsons, who are short on money because Mr. Johnson is laid off." "What is this kitchen table doing in the middle of the living room?" "Oh, that's for the Smiths, the missionaries who are home on furlough from Africa."

That's the way it always was. Mary's mom started collecting clothing and household items in her home for missionaries and the needy. Then what she collected became so plentiful, the Bensons' home couldn't contain it. So they moved the items to their church. Stores began to donate their unsold clothing to the effort, and the whole project eventually had to be moved to a warehouse. My mother-in-law called her ministry "The Repeat Boutique." The Repeat Boutique gave everything away from household items to clothing to computers, even cars. Thousands of missionary folks on furlough in Wheaton, Illinois and from all over the world have received help from the center, which is still in business today. Gaile would arrange to get the items and Stan would pick them up in his van. Many others began to volunteer for the work. It all became a huge success. Mary's parents donated not only their money but countless volunteer hours to the operation. If this wasn't amazing enough, the Bensons frequently had people living in their home and they never charged them a dime to stay there. There were foster children, college students, missionaries on furlough, and others. Gaile claimed that over the years at least a hundred different people had stayed in their home. When Mary and I were dating, Stan would often take the family, friends, and me out to a nice restaurant. He would always pick up the check for everyone. I would whisper my amazement to Mary, "Your dad paid for everyone, and he paid for me too!" It happened repeatedly, and it was so unlike my own dad. Mary's parents frequently had people in their home for dinner. They had tons of friends. Have you ever noticed that people who give a lot seem to have a lot of friends? My wife's parents gave plenty of money to their church and to missionaries. In their home they hosted Vietnamese refugees who had escaped from the Viet Cong at the close of the war in 1975. We got to know them well and to this day I can tell you their names (but I can't spell them). Mary's mom would often take needy people on assistance to government offices in Chicago where she would wait for hours for the clerical workers to process the paperwork. I had just never seen anything like this in my life. Their selfless example has made an indelible impression on my own practice of giving.

Stan and Gaile had no retirement savings and neither did they have a pension. So I kept wondering, "How is this all going to turn out when they get older and can't work any longer?" Instead of saving they gave and gave. Would they die in poverty? Well, the time did come and I saw firsthand what can happen to people who faithfully give to God's work and to the poor. Although they had no savings, Mary's parents did live in a wealthy suburb of Chicago where housing prices had escalated over the years. They had at least some equity in their home. They eventually sold it and moved to a retirement center near where we were living. The center was new and offered a deal that was later discontinued because it wasn't profitable for that facility. But Stan and Gaile got in when the going was good. The situation was that they could purchase for $130,000 their beautiful retirement condo, which had an attached two-car garage, vaulted ceiling, gas fireplace and more. It was really nice. They sold their house for about $230,000. Here was the good part: In addition to the price of the condo, the center charged $900 a month for rent. But at that time, they allowed renters to take that $900 a month out of the money they had paid for the unit. The price also included all utilities and taxes. So Mary's parents were able to live comfortably off their Social Security for the rest of their lives. Money was never a problem, and Stan would still take groups of people out for dinner and pick up the tab for the entire bunch. After they both passed away, Mary and her sister were each given a sum of $30,000 from their parents' estate. I saw that God's Word is true. He does provide for those who give faithfully.

I kept wondering, "How is this all going to turn out when they get older and can't work any longer?" Instead of saving they gave and gave. Would they die in poverty?

So Mary and I began to give generously through the little means that we had when we were first married. There were years when I was a youth pastor, and even as a senior pastor just didn't make much, but we always gave. Some years, taking the family to McDonald's was a real financial strain, but we always gave generously. We gave to the church, we gave to missionaries, and we gave to those who were in need. We never made a big deal about it, but we gave faithfully. I believe in giving anonymously when possible. Jesus criticized the religious hypocrites for making a show out of their giving. He accused them of blowing a trumpet before they put money in the temple treasury. Jesus said, "They have received their reward in full." He said, "Do not let your left hand know what your right hand is doing, so that your giving may be in secret. Then your Father, who sees what is done in secret, will reward you" (Matthew 6:3–4). I would rather be rewarded by God than by others any day.

So the big question is, how much are we supposed to give to the Lord's work and to those who are in need? We have all heard about tithing, which is giving ten percent. The principle of tithing comes from the Old Testament in the Bible. However, some have claimed that in the Old Testament, three tithes were actually required, and one of these was to be given every third year. I will leave biblical scholars to discuss that issue. We do know that although the tithe was an Old Testament principle, there is some indication that Jesus was in agreement with it.

Luke 11:42 tells us Jesus said, "Woe to you Pharisees, because you give God a tenth of your mint, rue and all other kinds of garden herbs, but you neglect justice and the love of God. You should have practiced the latter without leaving the former undone."

Note that Jesus seemed to chastise these religious leaders for their neglect of justice and their lack of love for God, but he told them that they were doing the right thing by tithing from all their income. Still, we would be hard pressed to claim the New Testament teaches that we must give an exact percent of what we make. Instead, there are general principles from it that guide our giving. I will point out just three of them.

A. Give Generously

"And now, brothers and sisters, we want you to know about the grace that God has given the Macedonian churches. In the midst of a very severe trial, their overflowing joy and their extreme poverty welled up in rich generosity" (2 Corinthians 8:1–2).

It is hard to define what it means to give generously. One single mom who lived in a trailer court and who was barely making ends meet told me, "Pastor, all I can give is one dollar a week. That's all I can afford." I told her what she was doing was fine because for her she was giving not only generously but sacrificially. For someone else giving a thousand a week would not be generous on the basis of the great salary he or she might be making.

Luke chapter 21 tells how Jesus and his disciples were in the temple watching people put their money in the offering bins. Some of the wealthy folks were making a big show of it as their many coins rattled in the offering containers. Suddenly, a poor widow put in two copper coins, but they hardly made a noise as she dropped them in the bin. People were impressed with what the wealthy were giving, but not Jesus. He was more impressed with the poor widow's contribution. He claimed she had actually given more than the wealthy folks, because they had given out of their wealth but she had given everything she had to live on. The struggling single mom from the trailer park was truly giving generously when she gave her dollar a week.

B. Give Proportionately

2 Corinthians 8:12 tells us, "For if the willingness is there, the gift is acceptable according to what one has, not according to what one does not have."

The woman from the trailer court was giving on the basis of what she had. But folks who give a thousand a week are not giving proportionately if they make a million dollars a year. This is where the concept of the tithe breaks down. For someone making a million dollars a year, giving their tithe is not enough because they still have $900,000 to live on. The poor single mom from the trailer court, in giving her dollar a week, had cut into living expenses. So we give according to our means. "To whom much is given, much is required." If we make a lot we need to give not only a lot more but a greater percentage of what we make.

C. Give Willingly

"For I testify that they gave as much as they were able, and even beyond their ability. Entirely on their own, they urgently pleaded with us for the privilege of sharing in this service to the Lord's people" (2 Corinthians 8:3–4).

These people, to whom the Apostle Paul was referring, were commended because they saw their giving as a privilege. They were willing to give. The major question is, "What kind of attitude do we have about what we give?"

On a Christian television program, a pastor was answering questions that people had previously emailed to him. One man wrote on how he was barely getting by financially but that somehow he had acquired an extra $900. The man wanted to know if he had to tithe on that $900. In my opinion, his attitude was wrong. To him, giving was drudgery, as it is for many people. "Oh, I don't know how I'm going to give any money. I can barely pay my bills now." Jesus said that it is better to give than to receive (Acts 20:35) and the writer of 2 Corinthians says that God loves a cheerful giver (9:7). Whatever percentage we give is between us and God but what isn't negotiable is our attitude. We are to give cheerfully and willingly.

"Bring the whole tithe into the storehouse, that there may be food in my house. Test me in this," says the LORD Almighty, "and see if I will not throw open the floodgates of heaven and pour out so much blessing that you will not have room enough for it" (Malachi 3:10).

Here's God's promise: If we give according to how he has instructed us, he will in turn bless us abundantly. This means not only spiritually but materially. I am not a prosperity Gospel preacher and I don't teach "seed faith", which proclaims, "If you give a hundred dollars to our television ministry, God's going to give you back a thousand. God wants you to drive a Cadillac and live in a mansion." That's not my style. On the other hand, I have seen how God has greatly blessed willing and faithful givers. My wife's parents are a prime example, and furthermore, I have seen it in my own life. I am convinced that my wife and I are in the good financial position we are in today mostly because of our faithful giving through the years. There have been some pretty lean times, but God has blessed and returned to us more than abundantly. People think God can't increase their financial situation because they are on a fixed income. Well, let me tell you, God can pour out the floodgates of heaven in ways that we could never imagine if we are faithful to him with our giving. Here's a case in point from my life:

As I have mentioned my wife, Mary, and I have been faithful in our giving since we were first married. A few years ago, Mary received a letter in the mail from a company that drilled for oil, and they wanted permission to drill on her grandfather's land in Pennsylvania. If we gave them the rights to the property, they would send us a check. It sounds like a scam, doesn't it, and I was skeptical. First, Mary never knew her grandfather. He had died before she was born. He was a somewhat successful businessman and had left a small amount to Mary's mom, but that money was long gone. Well, it turned out that the deal was legit and, unknown to us some property, or should I say some rights to a property, was still in her grandfather's name. In the end we received a check for $10,000. The incident reminded me that God can bless us abundantly even if we are on fixed incomes or even if we can't imagine where the money could possibly come from . He will do it if we give according to how he tells us to give.
Although the New Testament doesn't explicitly teach tithing in terms of an exact 10 percent, that is still is a good figure for many people to go by, especially for little guys like me who have small incomes. A millionaire should give a greater percentage but again, this book is written for the less affluent like you and me. Mary and I have always given 10 percent and there have been times when we have given more. I have a strict budget that we live by, but the giving category is the only category in which I want to exceed our spending limits. You've got to choose some percentage, so for many people the 10 percent is a good one. Studies have shown that Evangelical Christians are known for their giving. But it is

amazing how few church attendees actually give 10 percent to churches and charitable causes.

According to one study from George Barna Research, only nine percent of adults who consider themselves “born again” Christians give 10 percent of their income to the Lord’s work. This is less than 1 out of 10.

In my ministry, I have dealt with many people who were in bad financial shape. Some of them were making good salaries. In every case I can remember, the people who were in financial trouble gave almost nothing to God’s work. We need to give and we will be better off if we do. I heard a television minister suggest recently the 10, 10, 80 rule. Give 10 percent of what you make. Save 10 percent of what you make, and live off the 80 percent. For most of us this would be a very good rule. Many who are in bad financial shape would not be if they practiced it.

Chapter 8

Cut Expenses

I have read a lot of articles that suggest you need to have at least 1.5 million dollars in retirement savings in order to retire. Now, doesn't that make you feel sick inside? Especially since most of us, including myself, don't have nearly that much. Remember, this book is written to the little guy, like you and me. Those who have millions and millions can read a book by Warren Buffett. I saw an article that was titled "Can you retire on a mere million?" The article went on to say that a million dollars will give you only $40,000 of yearly income. That is really depressing. What can we do? One thing is to cut our expenses and learn to live more simply. Doing this is just as important as having a healthy retirement savings. If you have a $300,000 mortgage and are making payments on two new BMWs, and if you have a summer home in Florida and another getaway in Washington State, you can't retire on a mere million. But what if your small but comfortable house is all paid for and so is your car? What if you don't have any debt and you have cut the cable and have lowered your cell phone expenses? What if you don't own any vacation homes? What if, instead of going out to eat five times a week, you go out once a week or even once a month? What if you cut your expenses to $40,000 a year? How much would it take for you to live on? Well if you have the average amount of Social Security income of $2,800 a month (average per person is $1,400 per month) and if you have half a million in savings, withdrawing $20,000 per year (four percent), your yearly income would be $53,600. Suddenly things look a lot better, don't they? You'd be making $13,000 more than you'd be spending. I don't read articles that say you need a million or one and half million to be able to retire. It all depends on what your living expenses are. This will determine how much you need to have saved in order to retire.

Good Life Home Loans estimates the mean retirement income for 65-to-69-year-olds is $54,129 but drops to $46,797 for those 70 to 74. The Pension Right Center reports that half of all Americans 65 or older have incomes less than $24,224 per year. The Bureau of Labor Statistics reports that the average household spending for retirees is $45,756 per year. This may give you an indication of where you stand compared to other retirees.

You don't have to have $1.5 million to retire. You can live on a lot less if you are willing to cut your expenses. Some people just can't conceive of this because they have had a lifetime of spending lavishly. They would rather keep working way longer than they need to because they don't want to give up their uncontrolled spending habits, their compulsion for buying on credit, and their affluent lifestyles. It sounds a little bit like our federal government doesn't it?

Remember the last diet you went on? It was hard, wasn't it? It wasn't fun eating fruits and vegetables, going to the gym, and giving up Big Macs. So how long did your diet last before you went back to the old ways and put all those ugly pounds back on? For most of us, our diets last a couple of weeks or maybe a month or two at the most. The trick is learning how to make the new habits become part of your lifestyle instead of just a flash in the pan. For the few that do this, they have not only had to change their behaviors but the way they think about life. You've probably heard the expression, "Don't live to eat; instead, eat to live." It is an entirely different way of looking at food. Instead of using food as a source of comfort, think of eating only what you need to get through the day. Food is a necessary and enjoyable but overindulgence can bring great complications, as we all know.

.

Changing your eating habits for a lifetime takes tremendous

discipline and reliance on God. Food can be a terrible addiction and so can overspending. Some people just can't say no to bargains and sales and toys and bigger and more expensive stuff. Yet reckless spending is a way of thinking that has to be corrected if we are going to learn to live on less so we can retire on a smaller savings.

So we learn to enjoy what we have instead of constantly wanting what we don't have. We regularly give thanks instead of complaining about not having it as good as someone else has. On an episode of *The Andy Griffith Show,* someone, I can't remember who, bought a new four-door car. Seeing this, his friend sold his almost new car and also purchased a four-door car. When asked why he traded his almost new car for the newer one, the man said, "Because so-and-so is two doors up on me." I'm afraid that there are a lot of people worried about their friends being two doors up on them in one way or another.

So start to think about ways of cutting back, downsizing. Get rid of that two-story monster where you raised the kids. It's a money pit anyway, because of costly repairs and high utility bills. Buy a small ranch or a condo and consider moving somewhere that has reasonable taxes. Think of how you can cut back on monthly expenses. I haven't had cable or satellite for 10 years. I don't know what it costs, but I imagine you can easily spend $150 per month on one or the other or both. Just think what I have saved in 10 years at that price! That's a savings of $18,000 over a 10-year period. The same is true for cell phones. Some families pay a lot for their cell phone packages, but there are ways to save here also.

My wife and I pay a combined average of $30 per month for two smart phones. There are cheaper carriers; you just have to shop around. I look for the cheapest auto and home insurance and we only have one car. We don't have magazine or newspaper subscriptions. We eat out seldom and save a lot by eating the majority of our meals at home. I have known people who order in food every night. Imagine what that adds up to over time! We buy a lot of clothes from re-sale shops. You get the picture. It is possible if you are willing to discipline yourself and change the way you think, to get your expenses down to a level that will fall within a small but livable budget. Remember this: you can enjoy watching the ball game in your small den just as much as the rich guy does in his mansion. You can enjoy a good dinner in your modest kitchen just as much as a billionaire does in one of his many opulent homes. You can enjoy the beautiful trees in the city park just as much as the guy who lives on five acres. You don't have to own to enjoy. I enjoy driving through nice neighborhoods and looking at the expensive homes. But I'm glad I don't have to pay what it costs to live in them and maintain them. You can enjoy a lot on simple pleasures, and you can enjoy by observing. You don't have to own to enjoy something.

Remember this: you can enjoy watching the ball game in your small den just as much as the rich guy does in his mansion.

I used to live in a river town in southeastern Iowa. Keokuk, Iowa has some beautiful pre-Civil War homes set just off the Mississippi River. These home owners had some beautiful views. It was a little frustrating because their huge homes blocked the beautiful view of the river for the drivers and pedestrians. One day I saw a man sitting on his front porch on the non-river side of his beautiful home. I thought, "Now if I lived on the river, I would certainly not be sitting watching the street. I'd be sitting in the back taking in the beautiful view of the water." I don't know what the man was doing, but I imagine after a while he must have become a little bored with his beautiful view of the Mississippi. Here's my point: Don't think you have to own to enjoy. You can go to different parks and eye beautiful sights without having to try to purchase and maintain some monstrosity. In my city there are 75 parks consisting of 4,000 acres. I'm not confined to one view. I don't have to own anything. I can still enjoy by just gazing. I'm not limited to the same view that I might get bored with in time.

Part of my responsibility in my previous ministry as chaplain in a retirement center was to manage the Employee Assistance Program. Employees would come to me to apply for funds to help them with personal expenses that they couldn't meet. There were many who came over the 10 years of my employment and I noticed the following trends with many of the applicants: Almost all of them had expensive cell phones, cable TV plans, and car payments. They frequently ate out at fast food restaurants. I'm not saying this to condemn anyone, but to point out that often it's these little things that add up and put us over. We can live on a lot less if we learn to cut back on a lot of these unnecessary extras.

A. Drive Affordable Cars

My father believed that cars were a necessary evil, and he claimed that many people ruined themselves financially because they bought new and expensive automobiles. His relatives would joke that my dad just hated to buy a car, and it was true. When it had to be done, purchasing a car was not a happy event for him or the rest of the family. As I mentioned, we usually drove old clunkers. I remember an ancient car or two that were parked in the driveway. My dad was supposed to one day fix them but somehow he never got around to it, much to my mother's dismay. She finally insisted that he get rid of them. Miracle of miracles, my dad bought two brand new cars during his lifetime, a 1952 and a 1960 Ford. I can't imagine my father actually going against his tightwad principles and springing for a new car, much less two, but my mother had a powerful influence. Both of the cars were a piece of junk within a few years and I think they probably were when Dad bought them.

The engine on the Ford Fairlane had to be replaced the first year. As I remember, it bit the dust on our yearly trip from Chicago to Des Moines to visit my grandparents. I remember waiting at the Ford garage with my family somewhere off Interstate 80 between the two destinations.

I can't imagine my father actually going against his tightwad principles and springing for a new car, much less two, but my mother had a powerful influence.

My father had a good point, however. Some people do ruin themselves financially because of the cars they purchase. You might be able to easily get a car loan, but making the payments on that loan is another matter. There are a lot of people who have $500 to $700 car payments who simply can't afford them. Then, if your spouse works full time, which is quite possible, you can't have him or her breaking down on the highway. Better buy a second new one. See how some people sink themselves through cars? I have met many during my ministry who were being strangled financially by their high monthly auto payments. If you are in debt or if you want to downsize, you might consider selling the traveling money pit and purchasing a beater for a while until you can get things under control. Then, after you have saved the money, purchase the new or newer car in cash. You will save a lot on interest. By the way, if you purchase an almost new car, you can save a lot off the sticker price. Who cares if the car has 8,000 miles on it if you can save five or six thousand dollars? Also, I would recommend using internet programs that compare car prices. My last car I bought new because with this particular model, the new ones were cheaper than the used ones. This is because the used ones had a lot more options that I didn't need. So, using the internet I located a new car that was $5,000 less expensive than what the locals were charging for the very same model with the same options. It was well worth it for me to drive the three hundred miles to save that money. I will drive three hundred miles for you if you will give me $5,000 anytime. I also learned the benefit of purchasing new or almost new cars if you can afford them. I used to drive old beaters because it was all I could afford. Invariably they would break down in a few years. But the first new car (the one I bought to prove to my wife that I wasn't as stingy as she claimed) lasted 17 years, and it had very few if any costly repairs over that period. I had 269,000 miles on it and it didn't look too bad until my wife had an accident with it. I ended up giving the car to a young man who said he drove it until there were well over 300,000 miles on the odometer.

B. Simplify

It is through living simply that I get my reputation for being really cheap. My brother-in-law says there are three levels of being cheap. First there is cheap, then there is cheaper and below that there is Craig. That's true, except I believe a level exists under me, and that was my dad, Wilfred L. Burton. When my cheapness starts to get out of hand, Mary will say to me, "Now, Craig, don't be another Wilfred."

Truth be told, I don't like stuff, not too much of it, anyway. Just give me a few things and I'm happy: a small home with not too much clutter in it or I will start to get overwhelmed. My sister calls me a minimalist and it is true, I really am. My goal is not to get more stuff. I am always looking for ways to get rid of things. I'll tell you how this all came about.

I told you before that the Great Depression made an indelible impression on my parents. They just wouldn't throw stuff away. I wouldn't call them hoarders, but they had way too much for my comfort level. The three-story home I was raised in was filled with stuff from basement to attic. I already told you about the extra broken appliances that my dad had in the basement for parts. The two-car garage was filled with so much stuff my parents couldn't get the cars in. I would clean it out and organize it on occasion so at least they could get one car out of the elements. But in a month it would be back to messy normal. They also had a farm with a huge barn that was filled with old furniture, rusty farm equipment, and more. The house there was also filled with stuff as was the house they owned in the town near the farm. Then they had a trailer in Florida that was filled with things. This alone is enough to make anyone a stark raving minimalist, but what happened next really put me under.

I already told you that my wife's parents had a missionary closet, which grew into a warehouse of collected items to be given to missionaries and people in financial need. I wasn't a missionary but I was a pastor, and that was good enough for my mother-in-law. From the time we first got married until the time they were in their 80s, Mary's parents gave us stuff, stuff, and more stuff. They gave us all kinds of clothing, for not only the two of us but also for our three boys. Our house looked like a used clothing store, but the worst of it was the furniture. We're talking all kinds of furniture to add to the furniture we already had. Then there were tools for me and toys for the boys, and all of it was endless. I felt like I was physically and emotionally drowning in a sea of things. To preserve my sanity, I started giving things away and having garage sales. Garage sales are a good way to get people to pay you to haul away your junk. But my wife didn't see it this way. She would rescue furniture that I was trying to sell at the sales. I had to learn to sell things on the sly and she still, to this day, complains about the boys' rocking horse that I got rid of. "But, Mary, the boys are in their thirties now!" She complains about her bicycle that I sold even though she uses a walker and has severe balance issues. Well, you can see where my troubles began and why I have clutter-phobia. I get rid of stuff and don't want a lot of it hanging around, and now you know why.

How does all this relate to financial management? Well, if you have less stuff, you have fewer costs and less maintenance. Have you ever bought something only to discover later that you had one just like it at home that you didn't know you had? That's part of the problem of having too much stuff. If you have two homes, you have to furnish both of them, pay utilities on both of them, upkeep costs, taxes, and more. If you have two or three cars, your maintenance, insurance, and other costs double or triple. There are great advantages to living *simply.*

If you have less stuff, you have fewer costs and less maintenance.

My dad was my number-one financial hero, but he had far too many low-cost material things for my comfort. I would like you to consider the joy of living in a simple house, condo, or apartment where there just isn't room for a lot of complications. You will have fewer costs and things to take care of and worry about. All your friends may be remodeling their homes and adding expensive additions, which will raise their already high mortgages and property taxes, but you can live a simpler way. Years ago, many people with large families lived in little houses, and they had one car and few clothes and extras. They didn't have satellite dishes or cell phones or internet or dishwashers and microwaves, and they were completely happy. We can get by with a lot less than what we have. In fact, most of us can get by with about half our possessions and never miss them. In the retirement center where I recently worked I spoke with many residents who had lived in the same home for 40, 50, and even 60 years. During this time they did what we all do who own a house, they accumulated more and more stuff. There was stuff in their basement and attics, garage and the shed behind the garage. They had stuff they didn't know they had. But when they moved into the retirement center, they were forced to downsize and get rid of most everything. This is a good thing. It is a freeing thing. Although some of them missed their homes, I never met one who missed having all the stuff that they never really needed or used. Almost all believed it was a really good thing to downsize.

I'm telling you this because when we live in a smaller space and we learn to be satisfied with a lot fewer things, we can cut our expenses down. Remember, we're the little guys. We don't have a million and a half in our retirement savings. One of the ways that we can live on a fraction of that amount is to learn to live on less, thus helping to cut down our monthly expenses. Yes, you may be able to live on your Social Security even if you have a small amount saved in your retirement funds. But you have to be willing to cut your monthly expenses and commit to staying within a budget that fits into those expenses.

Living on the cheap can be a fun adventure. I don't know how much he makes now, but I have a friend who told me in one year he made over $400,000. I imagine he makes the same approximate amount now. The last time I saw him, he let me in on a little secret. He buys all his clothes at resale shops and so does his wife. They could buy their clothes anywhere but they think it is fun to buy nice clothes at a bargain. He likes to brag about his purchases.

"See this shirt, pretty nice huh? Well it cost me five bucks. See this sweater? It originally cost $100 but I got it at the Salvation Army for $10."

My father did that. I don't mean that he made $400,000 in a year or probably in a lifetime, but he loved buying secondhand clothes, as he called them. I remember sitting in the living room as a kid with my mother as my dad would model suits that he picked up at one of the city's resale shops. He strutted before us like a proud rooster, and he had a big grin on his face as he showed off his treasures. "See this one? I paid 50 cents for it. You like this one? It only cost me a quarter." So, it becomes a game to see if we can purchase things that others are paying two or three times more for.

However, let me raise this flag of caution. Even clothes bought cheaply can accumulate like rabbits and can bury a person in clutter. My dad had at least 75 suits—maybe 100—that had to be gotten rid of after he died. Does anyone need that many suits? It doesn't matter if a person buys new or used, too many clothes can clutter closets and basements and wherever you might be inclined to stash things. Now, speaking of my father's secondhand suits, there was one very tense marital moment that I witnessed because of them. It wasn't that my dad had too many to please my mom. She was just like him, except that she had tons of secondhand dresses instead of suits. But one day my mother was going through the pockets of one of his many suits, and she pulled out a deck of cards that had pictures of naked women on them. When my father got home that night he faced the inquisition. According to dad, the deck of cards with the naked women must have been in the pocket of one of the suits he had bought at the resale shop. As he said, "It had to be there before I even bought the suit and I didn't know it was there. That's my story and I'm sticking to it."

Let me raise this flag of caution. Even clothes bought cheaply can accumulate like rabbits and can cause clutter.

It would certainly have been out of character for my father to have in his possession such a deck of cards, so we all believed him. But I did learn one thing from this incident. When you buy used clothes, before you get home, always check the pockets. ,

Now, back to clutter because of having too many clothes. I am a man and I think like a man, but I have never quite understood a woman's reasoning when it comes to how many clothes she actually needs. Here's a familiar scenario, guys: Your wife has the double closet in your bedroom and it is over-filled with her clothes. Your few items of clothing are in a tiny wardrobe in the small bedroom that you are using for an office. Your tiny dresser is also there, because your wife's big dresser is in the master bedroom. She also has an additional dresser in the bedroom and this is why you have to put your tiny one in the second bedroom. In addition to the clothes in her stuffed double closet in the master bedroom there is a large wardrobe in the basement which holds her "off-season clothes." The living room coat closet is stuffed full with her many coats leaving barely enough room for your single jacket. My question is this: Why is it, when you are both getting dressed to go out, does she looks in her closet and sigh, "Oh, I have nothing to wear?"

Like I say, I am a man and I think like a man. But I've always wondered. . . . I'm in trouble aren't I?

One of the things I love to do is eliminate monthly expenses, or cut them down as much as I can. We've already talked about the high cost of cell phones and cable TV. There are ways to eliminate or greatly reduce the price of these. For example, we get about 30-some TV channels just through our antenna, and most of what we watch may be through streaming. We stream a lot of movies and Christian programs through YouTube and Amazon. I have not missed paying for cable channels and don't want to ever have to do it again.

What's more, there are a lot cheaper cell phone companies than the ones we hear advertized. Mint Mobile is the one we use and it costs us a fraction of what others pay for their phone service. A friend has Republic Wireless, and it too has cut his costs dramatically. Do an internet search and you will be pointed to similar plans. The same is true for a landline. A lot of people are getting rid of their landlines because they have cell phones. Others are still paying $50 or $60 a month for their services. For years I have used a company called Magic Jack, and I pay about $30 per year. I still enjoy a landline, but I'm not willing to pay what others are paying for service. I stay away from having monthly payments when possible whether for a car or lawn service or some program on the internet. These charges add up. For example, there are anti-virus computer programs you can pay a monthly fee for. But there are others that do the same thing for free. AVG and Avast are two of the most popular fee antivirus programs. There are password protection programs and utility programs that will cost you monthly. But others offer the same services for nothing. Daily newspapers and monthly periodicals are soon to be a thing of the past, but some people still subscribe to them. Hey, you can read a lot of the same stuff online. Many seniors are not into computers or the internet but they can still save money by sharing newspapers and periodicals with neighbors or by accessing the periodicals at the library._You can go to the library and read any magazine you want. Better yet, you can download books from the library to your streaming device. Stay away from monthly fees as much as you can because they can really add up. I do pay a monthly fee for a home security system, but it is necessary because of the neighborhood I live in. I only pay $24 a month, but my neighbor pays over $80 per month for hers. So shop around and avoid high monthly costs. Maybe you can't entirely eliminate all your monthly fees, but you can shop for cheaper options.

Chapter 9

Build Your Retirement Savings

So we've tracked our expenses and we've made a budget. We've cut down our monthly expenses and we've agreed to downsize and live simply. Now we've got to talk about our sources of income. The first thing we need to talk about is Social Security. As you know, a person can start drawing their Social Security beginning at age 62. But the longer you wait up till age 70, the larger your monthly payments will be. Every year you wait, your payment will increase by eight percent. Plus, if you're married you can collect a spousal benefit, which is half of what your spouse's Social Security payment would be if you wait. So, financial experts agree that it is wisest to wait until age 70 before collecting. One of the reasons for this is because people are living longer than they used to. When the first Social Security payments were issued in 1937, the average life expectancy in the United States was 61 years. Today, in 2020, the average life expectancy is 78.9 years. That is the average. I can tell you from working in a retirement center, there are plenty of people living into their 90s and many of these are in very good health. Some of these people have regretted collecting their Social Security payments starting at age 62. Almost all of the people in their 90s who have spoken to me about the subject have told me, "I never thought I would live this long." This is why it is wisest to wait until age 70 before collecting, and almost every financial advisor will suggest this.

However, there are two notable exceptions. If someone is in a financial jam, perhaps unemployed and on the verge of losing their home, they will obviously need to start collecting. The second reason for not waiting has to do with poor health. If someone is sick and can't work, or if he or she is having a difficult time working because of health reasons it might be wise to start collecting Social Security. Others are forced to start collecting because they have to stay home and care for a spouse who has health issues.

Some people, because of their poor health, feel that they probably won't live to 80, so why not start collecting? Figure what you would make by starting your payments at age 66 or whatever your full retirement age is, and calculate how long it would take your earnings starting at age 70 to match. This is your breakeven point. My breakeven point starting Social Security at age 66 would be age 82 or 83. Since my parents both died at age 69, and because of my wife's health issues, I started to collect my Social Security payments at age 66. I worked until I was 67 and saved every dime of my Social Security payments. This is one of the reasons I have such a sizeable cash savings. If you start collecting at your full retirement age, you can make as much money as you want and you're not penalized. If you start collecting payments before your full retirement age, you are only allowed to make so much money, or you will have to give back a certain amount. If a person can start collecting at their full retirement age and save every bit of their payments, they may be well ahead. My plan was to keep working until age 70 while saving my Social Security earnings, but certain factors led me to retire at age 67. If you do implement this strategy, have your employer take out of your check exactly what your Social Security payment will be and have him or her put it into your employee retirement savings. This way, you will not only have the benefit of your employer matching more of your funds, but you will save tremendously on income taxes. I paid only $2,500 on my federal tax return this past year because of implementing this strategy. As a married couple, you can put up to $27,000 into your 401(k) if you are over 50. For us little guys it would be nearly impossible to put away this amount, unless we did it by saving our Social Security payments as I just mentioned.

The solvency of Social Security needs to be considered. In other words, how long will it be around? When Social Security started, 41 workers supported one retiree. Today only 2.9 workers support one retiree. So many fewer workers support retirees because there are more elderly who are living longer. Social Security is projected to be fully solvent until the year 2033. After this time, Congress will either have to raise taxes or recipients will receive smaller amounts. While many think Congress will act the question is, will it be able to? Rising and uncontrolled federal deficits and the economic uncertainties brought upon by the COVID-19 pandemic are bringing about great financial fears. All of this has led some to think, *Should I start my Social Security payments while I can still get them?* Most financial advisors, however, say wait before collecting, believing that Congress will have to do something to build up the Social Security coffers.

When Social Security started, 41 workers supported one retiree. Today only 2.9 workers support one retiree.

The truth is, very few Americans can live off their Social Security alone. It is up to each of us to make sure we build a retirement nest egg. My father worked at the same job for over 30 years. He had something very few people have today, a pension. Because of this, he didn't have to do much financial planning in terms of retirement. All he had to do was continue his frugal way of living and he would be fine. This is not the case today. Either we will self-fund our retirement nest egg, or we will have little to exist on during our retirement years. As I said before, one-third of Baby Boomers have less than $25,000 put away for retirement. A major portion of people are going to be facing grave financial trials in the days to come. Another thing that has changed in our society is that families are not taking care of their elderly as they used to. Our elderly are placed in nursing homes and retirement centers, which has its good and bad points. We can't depend on our extended families to take care of us, making it all the more important to fund our own retirements. No one else is going to do it for us.

I was fortunate to be forced into beginning a retirement savings when I was 31 years old, although it is much wiser to start earlier than this. The church that I was a pastor at in rural Minnesota just automatically took money out of my check and put it into a retirement fund for me. They didn't even ask me. They just did it. At my young age, retirement seemed like a million light years away. But that little church got me started saving for retirement. This is something I would not have done on my own. When I started figuring my taxes, I learned that I could save a significant amount of money on what I paid the federal government if I would put money aside in an IRA. I could save twice that much on my taxes if I would also set aside money for my wife's Individual Retirement Account. So this was what I started doing every year. It was painfully hard to do on a small salary with three little boys, but I did it because of the tax savings. I love my country and my government but I'm not going to pay extra taxes if I don't have to. So this is how I began to fund my retirement savings. It started small, yet through consistently contributing over a long period of time and through wise investing, I was able to build up an adequate nest egg.

When I have spoken to young people in their 20s and 30s about the importance of saving for retirement, many think I am as crazy as a loon. Retirement seems to them many too many years away to even begin to think about it, much less save for it. We should begin to invest in our retirement as soon as possible, the sooner the better. Here is a little tidbit from the Vanguard website that shows the importance of starting early.

If at age 25 you put away $10,000 per year and do so until you are age forty and for some reason stop your contributions, you will have $1,058,912 at age 65. If your friend begins at age 35 and contributes the same amount of $10,000 until age 65 he will have accumulated $838,019. You will have put away approximately two hundred thousand more than your friend, although he has contributed for thirty years to your fifteen. This is due to the power of compound interest. The illustration assumes a four percent interest rate. You get the point; the earlier you start the far better off you will be.

If you are a person who loves to check the stock market daily and is fond of the joy of investing and studying finance, you are not going to need what I'm about to write to you next. I have a feeling most people are kind of like me what it comes to investing, however. I like to basically know what is going on, but I don't want to live there. I don't want to spend my life with my nose in the Wall Street Journal. I do, however, want to know enough to be able to manage my finances and have a good retirement.

A. Learn about Investment Basics

So let's start with some basics about investing and saving for a comfortable retirement. Keep in mind there are myriads of investment vehicles that I won't mention because I just want to focus on some simple ones that the majority of retirees are invested in. We're going to start with some really easy concepts. First let me say, although people make money through investing in art, real estate, antiques, and so on, I'm going to speak only of financial investing. Other investment tools are higher risk and I don't have the knowledge or interest to get involved in them. My dad was more courageous than I and bought a farm when he was 52 years old. It turned out to be a great investment for him, but at the time it was risky. He had a family and a home, but he took the risk and it worked out really well. I am more conservative, and I take a lot fewer risks than my father did. You have to figure out your "risk tolerance" as you think about how you are going to invest. I know people who have lost their shirts through real estate investing, but there are many others who have made money. You have to figure out what your comfort level is. As one conservative investor told me, "I want to be able to sleep at night." I would not advise investing in non-traditional methods unless you are one that can handle the ups and downs that will result.

An article by Blake Ellis in *CNNMoney* describes 11 Crazy Alternative Investments. Ellis tells how people emptied their 401(k)s to invest in more non-traditional sources. These included antique raffles, dressage horses, ostrich farming, raising Christmas trees, and vodka distilleries. Some of the investments were quite bazaar. One man took his retirement savings and invested in chicken feces that he sold to fertilizing manufacturing companies. Another man socked his entire $300,000 retirement nest egg into raising organic sprouts. His company has 16 different types of sprouts that grow in nutrient rich water instead of soil. At the time the article was written, the company employed 15 people and the man had made a 100% return on his initial investment (Ellis, Blake "Retirement Savings Near All-time High," *CNNMoney,* July 1, 2011, 1:56 p.m., July 5, 2011, 2:46 p.m.). Someone might be able to make a financial killing in these unorthodox retirement investments, but do you really want to risk your entire retirement on something so uncertain? Go for more traditional investments that have had a solid track record. The stock market is admittedly risky, but if you are well diversified you should be able to weather financial downturns over the long term.

1. Bank Accounts

You should have a savings as well as a checking account. It is surprising how many don't have a savings. You know how your bank gives you interest for using your money and how each account is federally insured. The problem is that bank accounts pay such terribly small interest. When my mother retired, her banks were paying so well, she could live off her interest and never have to touch her principle. If that was the case today, I would move my investments to banks in a heartbeat. But it is not the case, so we have to look elsewhere. There are some checking accounts that pay a higher interest if you keep a minimum balance and have a set amount of debit charges per month. I make $50-70 each month off my checking account. See Bankrate.com or NerdWallet.com for competitive rates.

2. Certificates of Deposit

These take your money for a set period of time and pay you a set interest somewhat higher than a savings account. The ones offered by banks pay a lower interest than private companies. The disadvantage of certificates of deposit is that your money is tied up when you might need it later on. If you take it out before the C/D matures, you'll pay a hefty penalty. Some people ladder their C/Ds so *that* they mature on different years. This is a good plan for a conservative investor.

3. Money Markets

With a Money Market, you give a company your money, and they give you interest that fluctuates. They usually pay less than C/Ds, but they're liquid. You can take them out anytime without penalty. Money Markets through banks usually pay less than private companies.

Although savings accounts, C/Ds, and Money Markets issued through banks are about as safe as you can get, even the highest paying ones don't match inflation. You are basically losing money because interest rates are so low today. Bank accounts are insured by the federal government, FDIC up to $250,000 per account. But at the time of this writing, banks pay very low interest on savings and money markets. The low interest rates lead us to consider the financial markets that fluctuate greatly but over the long run can offer a substantial rate of return depending on what you invest in. An investor needs to consider the issue of risk verses reward. Usually safe investments especially ones backed by the federal government pay very little interest. If you want to make more money you will have to risk more including the money you have in your principle (initial payment that you invest). Your C/D may be safely insured and you don't have to worry about losing the money you invested in it. But it pays very little in terms of return. If you risk your principle in more aggressive types of investments, you are often times able to make more money. But you can also lose more money. It is all a matter of risk verses reward. The more you risk the more you make but your investment isn't as safe. If you want to play it safe, go with a money market, a savings or a certificate of deposit. You just won't make very much by going this route. That's why a person has to figure out their risk tolerance. Some are fine investing heavily in the financial markets and others will lose sleep if they do so.

4. Stocks

Stocks are financial units that make up a company. You can purchase these units (shares) in a company, and you will own that part of the company you are invested in. If the stock goes up in value, you will make money. If you would have invested $1,000 in Amazon stocks in 1997, it would be worth $1, 341,000 in 2018. Now don't we all feel sick? I don't invest in individual stocks because they are too volatile. You can make a lot but you can lose a lot as millions did during the 1929 bust and in other times of financial collapse. As I have said, the object is not to get rich but to have a comfortable retirement through wise conservative investing. Always operate from this perspective. I would not advise putting a lot of your money on a fast horse. Go for the conservative long-term approach to investing. You won't get rich, but you will be able to be comfortable in retirement. This, again, is the goal.

5. Bonds

When you buy a bond, you give the company your money and they issue you periodic financial payments. After the bond matures, they give you back what you originally gave them. Some bonds are fixed and some rise and fall with market conditions. Some pay higher returns but are more risky. Usually the lower the risk, the lower your return is. Keep in mind there are many kinds of bonds. Bonds tend to be more secure during times of economic collapse. Some of them even made money during the collapse of 2008. But generally, bond markets as well as stocks tanked during that year. Bonds also go down as interest rates go up.

6. Mutual Funds

A mutual fund has stocks and bonds and other types of investments in it. It is managed by an individual or a group of managers. Because the funds need to be managed, it costs more to own than individual stocks or bonds. But because managers can change the fund components according to market conditions, they are more stable than individual stocks and bonds. There are 9,599 mutual funds and approximately 17.71 trillion dollars invested in them. Some of them are front load, meaning that you pay a price to invest in the fund; some of them are rear load, meaning that you pay the price when you sell it. I would not invest in anything but a no load fund. Some companies, like Vanguard and T. Rowe Price, offer nothing but no load funds. However, the expense ratios (what they actually charge to manage your fund) can vary greatly. By and large, Vanguard is much cheaper than T. Rowe Price when it comes to the cost of managing mutual funds. Over a period of time the expense ratio of mutual funds can make a dramatic difference in earnings. For small investors who don't want to spend a lot of time researching and managing individual stocks and bonds, mutual funds are a great way to go.

7. Annuities

Annuities are offered by insurance companies. You give the company your money and they give you a set rate of return. Annuities are like bonds, except that the money you give them never comes back to you, only the interest. They can be good for part of your financial portfolio, but I would not put a large portion of your money in them, because they don't adjust for inflation and they are not liquid. If you need the $100,000 that you gave them, you cannot get it back. You will only get the interest. Right now is a terrible time to invest in annuities because interest rates are so low. I have a friend, however, who years ago bought an annuity that gives her eight percent on her returns. Today you would get a lower interest rate and it would remain fixed. Once you purchase an annuity, it belongs to the company. Annuities can offer peace of mind because you know that you will always receive a set amount of return no matter what. This is important for some investors. These investments will only tank if the insurance company you purchased them from goes under. This is why the insurance companies are rated so you can sense how secure they are. A.M. Best gives a rating to each insurance company. An A+ or A++ is a superior rating. An A or A- is an excellent rating. A good rating is B+ or B++. Ratings go all the way down to D, which is poor. Lower rated companies offer greater returns but at higher risk. There are different kinds of annuities. Some are immediate and some start paying at a future date. There are also variable rate annuities which are based on the stock market. I would strongly suggest staying away from them. They are complicated and will require that you pay a hefty commission to a salesperson. I have never read anything positive about variable annuities except from the companies that sell them. As a rule, don't invest in something you don't understand, and variable rate annuities are difficult to understand. Returns are often not what they lead you to believe they will be.

As I said, there are many other types of investments--government securities are one of them--but they pay very little, even though they are secure and are backed by the United States government. The first investments we talked about (savings, C/Ds, money markets) are pretty easy to understand. They just don't pay you much in returns. So that forces us to look into the financial markets, and for me, I would stick with mutual funds as opposed to individual stocks, although it is possible to do well if you bet on the right horse, so to speak. But as I mentioned, that is not the purpose of what we are trying to do. If you do purchase individual stocks, make sure that they are a small part of your portfolio and that you won't need the money for years to come. Because if you need the money from your stock in the near future you will suffer a great loss if it's value goes down dramatically.

8. *Individual Retirement Accounts (IRAs)*

My dad and many of his generation had a pension. It was not necessary for him to lay money from his paycheck aside to fund his own retirement. Pensions were a great benefit for many American workers but because people are living longer today, they have almost become a thing of the past. Many companies could not afford to continually pay out pensions because of it. So the government has allowed for people to set up their own private retirement or Individual Retirement Accounts. All money that goes into IRAs is tax deferred, meaning you don't pay taxes until you withdraw from your retirement account. The great advantage is that the government gives a break on your yearly income taxes if you contribute to your IRA. If you are under 50, you can contribute $6,000 yearly into an IRA and $7,000 if you are over 50. The same amounts can be contributed by your spouse. By making the full contribution, I have saved about $1,500 on my taxes. (It varies year to year.) That is $1,500 less that I have to pay Uncle Sam. The money in your IRA accumulates and can grow significantly over the years. The downside of an IRA is that it takes great discipline to make these contributions. It is like going to the gym. It's a great idea, but most don't have the discipline to do it consistently over a long period of time.

The downside of an IRA is that it takes great discipline to make these contributions. It is like going to the gym. It's a great idea, but most don't have the discipline to do it consistently over a long period of time.

Roth IRAs are a better choice than traditional IRAs because although you don't get the tax break initially, you won't pay taxes when you retire. The money in your traditional IRA is tax deferred, meaning it will be taxed when you take it out. But there will be no taxes on your Roth But here's why I don't have any Roth IRAs: Through years of tight budgets, raising a family, and barely getting by sometimes, I would never have been able to sacrifice and put money away unless the government offered me an immediate tax break. In other words, if I hadn't received that $1,500 off my taxes, I never would have put the money in my retirement account. It was either a traditional IRA contribution or nothing. I just wouldn't have gone the Roth route. Many are in the same boat as me. So although Roth IRAs are a better choice, they are extremely hard for most people to take advantage of without the immediate tax advantages that a traditional IRA offers. By the way, the $1,500 I saved may not be what you save by contributing to your IRA. It depends on your financial situation.

B. Choose Financial Advisors Wisely

So where do we begin knowing which mutual funds to purchase? We go to a financial advisor and there are all sorts of them. There is huge money to be made in services to seniors, because the Baby Boomers are retiring and there are so many of us. Financial advisors are well aware of this and are eager to cash in on the situation. I don't mean that in a negative way, although there are some piranhas out there. Some advisors will give you financial advice for a set fee. Others want to sell you something with their advice. If they want to sell you something, they will be looking to offer you products that give them greater commissions. For this reason, I would suggest staying away from dealing with advisors who peddle financial products. It is just too tempting for them to have ulterior motives. Never go to anyone who is not a fiduciary. A fiduciary is a financial advisor who has your best interest in mind. Many advisors also want to manage your retirement investments. They are good for someone who doesn't want to think or worry about their investments. "Just keep the checks coming and let me know if there is a problem." Financial managers can also hold your hand during financial downturns. "It's all right; don't panic, don't sell--the markets will come back." The emotional support is important because the last thing we want to do is sell when the market drops. Many people did this in 2008. But the markets did come back and eventually people who didn't sell got their money back. Those who did sell lost out on the market gains of the coming years. The old saying of "buy low and sell high" is very true. A financial manager can remind us of this during market downturns when we are beginning to panic. If your advisor is an accountant, he or she can give you important tax advice that can save you thousands of dollars.

I don't use a financial manager, and the reason is because of the costs involved. Most financial managers charge between one and one and a half percent to manage your funds. That doesn't seem like much until you do the math. One percent of a million dollars is $10,000, and it is paid yearly. In 10 years you have paid your financial manager $100,000 to "manage your retirement funds". Plus, studies have shown that managed funds don't in the long run beat index funds. Index funds are not managed but just rise and fall according to the stock markets. Vanguard has built a kingdom and a reputation for their successful index funds that cost almost nothing to invest in.

Most financial managers charge between one and one and a half percent to manage your funds. That doesn't seem like much until you do the math.

A wealthy resident from the retirement center where I served was known for his generous giving. There is a hallway in the new building named after him. He told me once that he gave $70,000 to both of his nephews just because he wanted to. He has given a lot of money to the city's cemeteries, which were his passion. When the governor visited our facility, he asked about the man by name. The resident had a reputation for his generosity. I asked him one day about his investment philosophy. He told me that he had no financial manager, but only invested in one Vanguard Index Fund. I asked him, "Yeah, but don't you need to diversify?" He said that the fund already is diversified. By the way, the man was not a businessman or a real estate developer. He was a junior-high history teacher. How much managing does it take to put your money in some low-cost index funds from a reputable company?

I also read that many financial managers never look at their customer's portfolios until the night before they are coming in for their yearly review. This is not encouraging, but it was a financial manager who made the claim.

Many companies have 401(k)s that are a small, selected group of funds to which you designate your retirement funds. You tell your employer how much from your paycheck you want them to put into these funds. Many companies will match what you put in up to a certain percent. This is an incredible deal. Not only are you making money on your fund earnings, but from your employer's free contributions. I would put as much as you possibly can into this unbeatable deal.

Now, this is where I believe it is dumb to have a financial manager. It is very easy to decide which 401(k) funds you should invest in. Let's say you only have 13 funds to choose from in your 401(k). How difficult can it be? You can read on the internet what your allocation should be for your age. If you are young, you want to highly invest in equities (stocks), and if you are older you want to have much more in bonds. The closer you get to retirement, the safer you want the lion's share of the funds in your portfolio to be. Most 401(k)s offer fixed investments that are like a savings account. They pay a set interest amount, and this amount is not affected by how the markets perform. As I got closer to retirement, I put a huge proportion of my 401(k) into this fixed alternative. A financial advisor suggested that I put 50 to 60 percent of my 401(k) and my total portfolio into equities. I am so glad I didn't listen to him, because the week after I retired the markets dropped dramatically due to the pandemic. I would not have been able to retire if I had done what he said, and many who were getting ready to retire but would not be able to because they were invested too highly in equities. However, the markets did come back after their initial drop due the pandemic. So looking back now, I realize that I would have made a lot more money if I had put 50 or 60% of my portfolio into stocks or mutual funds. But on the other hand I realize that the market could tank again and I wouldn't want to be in a position to lose all that money. So I am content with my conservative plan and I am able to sleep at night. We have to all determine what our personal tolerance for risk is.

Make sure that as you grow closer to retirement age you are more invested in safer investments, not in those more volatile, like stocks. You don't need to pay a financial manager thousands of dollars a year to tell you how to invest in the small number of funds in your 401(k). You can figure this out yourself. Remember this, if the market drops dramatically you have not only lost the value of your investments but the fees your manager is charging you. In order to make money even in good times, you have to make more than what the manager is charging you. So, if he or she is charging you one percent, you have to make at least that just to break even. Again, financial managers have their place, especially for people who don't like to fool around with their investments. Often older people have a difficult time managing their financial affairs on their own. But in many cases, it is not difficult to invest if you stick with simple options and a simple plan.

1. Out to Lunch

You can get free investment advice from financial advisors, many of whom offer free lunches to people who will sit through their sales presentations. I have attended four or five of these and have found them well worth my time. These advisors usually want to manage your investments. This is their ultimate goal. They give you a free lunch and they share a lot of information, but they really want to manage your portfolio. From what they charge, you can see why they want to do so. Instead of having a financial manager, I decided to go it on my own. I've learned a lot just from reading articles on the subject of personal finance and retirement. There is a lot out there if you are willing to take the effort to learn. Other advisors offer a free one-time session to anyone seeking retirement advice. I have been to several conferences and have learned a lot in the process.

2. Robo-Advisors

Some major investment companies like Fidelity, Charles Schwab, and Vanguard offer Robo-Advisors, which basically means they use computers and logarithms to figure out where you should invest. The cost is about a third of what a standard human financial advisor usually charges. They also advise you on getting tax advantages when you sell investments. The really good thing is that all of these companies offer hybrid programs that combine Robo investing with a human being. In many cities, Fidelity has offices in which you can directly speak with investors in the flesh. In most cases you will speak with different advisors on the phone, but if you have $500,000 or more invested with Vanguard, they will give you a designated advisor. It sounds like a really good way to go, and it is a good way to receive professional investment advice at a fraction of the cost of a traditional manager. Keep in mind that all three companies want you to purchase their products. If you have enough invested in Vanguard, they will also give you advice regarding the money you don't have with their company, such as what is in your 401(k). All these companies have great websites where you can read good articles on retiring and investing.

The really good thing is that all of these companies offer hybrid programs that combine Robo investing with a human being.

It is also easy to move your money from one fund to another through the websites if you have an online account. It is difficult, however, to move your money from one company to another. For example, if you want to move all or some of your money from your 401(k) to Vanguard, there is a lot of paperwork and in some cases you have to get medallion signature guarantees and signatures by notaries. I just went through this, and it takes a lot of time and patience. Some people think this process is difficult because companies don't want you to move your money out of their funds. The paperwork is a way of discouraging investors from doing this. Although it is difficult to move your funds from company to company, it is very simple to move your funds within a company. For example, if you have your investments with Vanguard, you can easily get on your account website and move your money from fund to fund.

The same is true with most 401(k)s. It is a very easy process to move your funds around online within your 401(k) choices. Robo investing is a good way to go, and if you like the human touch you can go with the hybrid approach. If you are connected to your company's website through your own account, you can get a bird's-eye view of all your money and move it around as you like. Having access to your funds by computer combined with Robo investing services can usher you into state-of-the-art convenient investing.

On an old TV commercial, Dallas Cowboys owner Jerry Jones asked the multi-sport talented athlete, Deion Sanders the following questions: "Which is it going to be Deion, baseball or football?" Sanders replied, "Both." Then Jones asked him, "What's it going to be, 40 or 50 million?" Again Sanders replied, "Both." The second reply left the Cowboy's owner with an astonished look on his face.

For you, when it comes to retirement savings, you can do both. You can have your employer make contributions from your paycheck into your 401(k) and you can make your own contributions into your IRA. Restrictions apply, but I have been able to do this for several years. Most people think they could not afford to do both but it becomes possible if you have enough cash reserve. For example, if you have $100,000 in personal savings, it is not hard to contribute to your IRA even if you have given to your 401(k). Whichever retirement vessel you use, just make sure you do it. Most people put it off, and that's why they have nothing saved for retirement. That to me is tragic because someday, even if we love our jobs, most of us are going to want to or have to retire.

Someday, even if we love our jobs, most of us are going to want to or have to retire.

When I was in junior-high school, the entire class was given six months to work on a science project that we were to present to the class. The project would make up the majority of our grade. I didn't think about it much until literally two or three nights before my project was due. Crying, I woke my father up in the middle of the night, confessing my dilemma. Fortunately for me, he stayed up with me for two nights making a crystal radio set, which I was able to present as my science project. The radio never worked but by God's grace the teacher never asked me to turn it on and never queried its usefulness. The anxiety I suffered because of my neglect taught me the valuable lesson to not procrastinate. It is never good to put off things you know you have to do, and this is especially true when it comes to making retirement contributions. Don't put it off. Even if you can only make small contributions, they will accumulate in time.

C. Diversify

Because my father lost his life savings during the Great Depression, he refused to put all his eggs in one basket. As I mentioned, when I became the executor of my parent's estate, I discovered small amounts of money stashed away in quite a few banks. Now that bank accounts are FDIC insured up to certain amounts, it is not as necessary to have many bank accounts. It is still a good idea to diversify, however. If you have all your money in mutual funds that are mostly invested in stocks, you will take a beating if the stock market drops dramatically as it did in 2008 and 2020. There are many people about to retire in 2008 who could not because their investments were not diversified, and the same may be true for future market collapses.

My neighbor lost a lot of his retirement funds in 2008 and said he would never again put any money in the stock market. Unfortunately, he withdrew it and not only took a financial beating but missed out on all the market gains in the years that followed. In contrast, if you have some money in stocks and some in mutual funds, some in cash, some in CDs and some in bonds, some in silver and gold, some in real estate, and so on, you will be better protected when one or two of these investments begin to tank. For example, if stocks drop, you will still have money in bonds and CDs to offset this loss. This is where a good financial/retirement advisor can help. He or she can walk you through diversification options and advise you when to sell, purchase new investments, and/or rebalance your portfolio.

D. Allocate Properly

On the other hand it isn't too hard to figure out how you should proportion your investments, if you want to manage your portfolio yourself. You can find suggestions through investment companies and through looking on the internet. For example, one source suggests that a 50 year old should have 8.5 percent of his or her portfolio in stocks, 10 percent in bonds and five percent in other investments. Other sources suggest you subtract your age from 110 and that number should be the percentage you invest in stocks and the rest is what you should invest in bonds. So if you are 50 years old, you should have 60 percent in stocks and 50 percent in bonds. If you are 60 years old, you should have 50 percent in stocks and 60 percent in bonds. When I am speaking of stocks and bonds, I am speaking mostly of mutual funds that are made up of either. Also keep in mind that mutual funds can be made up of a combination of individual stocks and bonds and other investments. Some mutual funds are more highly invested in stocks and some are more highly invested in bonds. You can read about what a mutual fund is made up of and about its past performance in the investment company's website as well as through the fund's prospectus. The later is very long, technical, and boring reading—helpful however, for insomniacs.

1. The Bucket Approach

Another tool to help you decide how to allocate your funds is the "bucket approach," which has many variations to it. This is how a financial advisor explained it to me: Bucket number one holds money that you will need in the next 1-5 years. This covers cash in your checking and savings accounts, money market funds, emergency fund, and the like. This is money you can get at now if you need it. Bucket number two holds the money you will need in the next 6-10 years. It consists of things like CDs and bonds including government bonds. Bucket number three has money you won't need for 11 to 15 or more years. This is comprised of individual stocks and mutual funds. The securities in this bucket should be higher risk, offering higher potential returns. The percentage that you have in each bucket depends upon your age. Just as a person should have more in bonds and less in stocks the closer they get to retirement age, a person should have more in bucket one and two and less in bucket three as they get into their late 50s and 60s. Here's the great benefit of the bucket approach: You never have to worry. I use the bucket approach, and even though the market has tanked because of COVID-19, I have just a small amount invested in bucket three. Almost all of my investments are in buckets one and two. Drops in the stock market don't faze me a bit because I am well secured in liquid funds (funds that I can get at right away). But if a person has almost everything in bucket three and very little ready cash, market disasters spell personal disasters. This is why today, as I write this, many are waiting in food lines. Because their places of employment shut their doors quickly due to the pandemic, many were in dire straits. They had nothing in bucket one, no emergency fund, no savings, and when the unthinkable happened they were in deep trouble. Some of these may have had money in bucket three, maybe they had retirement savings, 401(k), and IRAs, but the funds were not available when they needed them. In my opening statements I said that a financial advisor, after reviewing my portfolio, claimed that I was in better shape than anyone he had spoken to in two or three years. It was not because of the amount of money in my portfolio, but rather in the way that I have it allocated. He said that I was already invested in the three-bucket approach, although I didn't realize it at the time.

A lot of those who work in the financial field recommend having an emergency fund that will cover two or three months of living expenses. I would suggest at least a year's worth in an emergency fund. I have known people who were unemployed for well over a year. It is better to play it safe. The current times present a lesson for those who live from paycheck to paycheck. We need to be prepared for a financial setback. We just don't know what can happen in the future. Establishing a well funded emergency fund is a must. Some people cannot save money. If they get a little money they are quick to spend it. Saving is a discipline that must be acquired. It came easier for me because of my father's example, but so many people need to learn to save in spite of not having positive examples.

2 Target Funds

Target funds are great tools for those who don't want to have to go to the trouble of rebalancing their portfolio. The fund manager does it for them. Target funds have a year associated with them, usually the year the investor wants to retire. The closer you get to that retirement year, the more the fund managers put into bonds and the less they put in to equities (stocks). So the investor doesn't have to make the effort of figuring out how much to allocate into different categories. The fund managers do the work for them. I have all of my wife's IRA funds invested in a Vanguard 2020 target fund. I can just leave it there and not worry about it. Keep in mind, the cost of maintaining a target fund is more than it costs to maintain funds like index funds, which do whatever the markets do. This is because there is more work involved for the manager. Target funds are also less volatile. During a crash they will drop, but not as much as an equity fund because they are protected with a greater percentage of bonds.

3. *My Personal Approach*

Here is the way that I've allocated my funds. I have about 78 percent of my funds in cash or fixed interest-bearing funds. I have about 14 percent in stocks and about eight percent in bonds. I mentioned before that an advisor encouraged me to have 50 or 60 percent of my funds in stocks. I am glad I didn't listen to him. No one anticipated the great pandemic of 2020 and the extreme drop in the markets. The money I have in cash (bucket one) and in CDs and bonds (bucket 2) are low interest bearing. But I don't care about the low interest; at least I haven't lost hundreds of thousands of dollars due to the collapse of the financial markets. When you are young and when retirement is decades away, put a good portion of your money in aggressive funds, meaning funds that have a potential of high earnings with a higher degree of risk. If the markets go south you will have potentially many years to recover. But if you are aggressively invested when you are 65 and the market tanks, you are in sad shape and may have to delay your retirement indefinitely. It can take a long time for financial markets to rebound from a serious downturn.

I have read many articles on retirement over the last few years. One in particular resonated deeply with me and spoke to what I felt I needed to strive for. The author said basically, don't try to make a killing and don't be aggressively invested. Instead, strive to live off the interest of your investments during your retirement years. I remember my mother telling me that she was doing this when she retired. Now, this was back in the years when banks were paying high interest on safe investments and it was possible for a person to do exactly this. I thought at first that it would not be possible to do in today's financial conditions. But as I examined my situation carefully, I discovered it is possible to live off my earnings without touching my principle. I could do this by keeping a sizeable amount of my retirement portfolio in a financial vehicle that paid fixed interest. I could combine this interest with what I made through Social Security. As long as I keep my living expenses low, I can manage without having to touch my principle. The alternative to this approach is to invest 50 to 60 percent of your retirement savings in equities balanced with the rest in bonds. Then the traditional thinking is to withdraw four percent a year from your portfolio when you begin to retire. If all goes well, you should be able to have your money last 30 or so years and, hopefully, until you die. But if the market goes through extended bear years (when the stocks drop at least 20 percent), maybe your funds will only last twenty years. There are web calculators that will compute how long your funds last as you enter in your financial variables. This approach didn't set well with me because I know from working with retirees over the past 10 years, that one of the greatest fears they have is running out of their money. So I like the approach of living off your earnings and not touching your principle. It can be done if you budget carefully and keep your living expenses low. If folks can do this, they will have fewer worries about running out of their money.

I like the approach of living off your interest and not touching your principle. It can be done if you budget carefully and keep your living expenses low.

Most 401(k)s offer a fixed alternative in which you can receive a set amount of earnings, maybe two to four percent. If you know what your expenses are going to be and how much you will receive from Social Security and other fixed sources (like pensions), you can figure out what your gap is. Your gap is the money you need to cover what these other regular sources of income can't. It may be that your interest from the fixed portion of your 401(k) can cover this gap. If it does, you won't have to touch your principle unless something unforeseen happens, like medical catastrophes or having to go into a long-term medical facility. Barring something like this, I believe living off your interest or dividends combined with Social Security is a good way to go. The goal is not to make a killing in the market or to strike it rich but rather to live well, within your means. It is a conservative, worry-free approach to retirement.

E. Keep Track

A farmer who attended the church I was pastor of in rural Minnesota bought quite a few cows in Missouri as an investment. The problem was that the cows were too far away for him to manage properly. He not only lost the cows, but he jeopardized his entire farming operation in Minnesota. He told me he learned that "if you have cows, you better take care of them or they will take care of you." The same truth for taking care of cows applies to taking care of our money. If we don't watch our budgets carefully, we will overspend. If we don't discipline ourselves to save money, we will be up a creek without a paddle when a crisis comes. How can we watch our investments, track our spending, plan for retirement in a manageable way? While I wouldn't use the word "easy," I would describe the process as simple and doable if you have the right tools. You could use a pencil and paper to do all of this, or you could take advantage of state-of-the-art computer and web-based financial technology. A farmer could do his field work with a mule and a plow and it would work, but how much better to use planters, tractors, and combines.

Most likely your bank allows you to pay your bills through their website, and you can even categorize your expenditures. Two popular web-based programs are Mint (which is free) and Personal Capital (which has a free option). Mint is good for tracking expenses and setting up a budget. It is not so good for tracking investments. Personal Capital has a free version and one you pay for that offers more features. Personal Capital is known for its great investment tools. It can analyze how much you are actually paying to your financial company for managing your mutual funds. Both programs excel on mobile platforms, which appeals to younger folks who spend more time on their phones than on their personal computers.

Quicken is the grand-daddy of them all. It was one of the earlier software financial management programs and I personally have used it for years. It tracks your expenses, helps you create and maintain a budget, and lets you see your investment allocation. It helps you plan for retirement and reminds you of upcoming bills. Through Quicken, you can easily pull up reports such as expense versus income or budget reports. It has tax assistance, and you can pay bills directly through its Quick Pay and Check Pay services. Best of all, it lists all your accounts, bank accounts, investments, credit card, and it allows you to get a bird's eye view of everything in one glance. Click on the one-step update, and it will download your latest transactions, including expenditures and earnings. You are constantly kept abreast of what you have and what you owe and your accounts are always balanced. If there is any fraud or questionable expenses on your accounts, you will be the first to know. Quicken also informs you of your updated credit score. The program has some weakness; you must pay every year or you will be unable to use its online services, which I think are critical. The program is kind of old school as more programs are web based and are intended for a mobile platform. It does have a mobile app, but that doesn't have all the functions of the computer program. I also don't recommend putting your financial information on your phone. If you lose it, someone could hack your information. I feel that Quicken is a good tool for taking care of your cows or, I mean, your financial matters before they take care of you. If I was just starting out, I would look into one of the free financial programs--after all, I am Wilfred Burton's son, and Cheap, I mean Free, is my middle name.

Chapter 10

Avoid Obstacles to Successful Retirement

There a lot of threats to ruining someone's financial freedom and security and their ability to retire when they want to. I'd like to spend quite a bit of space discussing them, because these obstacles can absolutely ruin one's financial situation and retirement prospects.

A. Reckless Spending

By far this is the number one obstacle that keeps people in poor financial straits. Some people are just addicted to spending. They can't grasp the idea that their spending has limitations. So they are constantly buying things on credit and are always accumulating more debt. As long as they can get approved for a loan, they think they can afford it. Someone called a financial radio program host complaining that they were in debt and couldn't make ends meet. The caller wanted to know if the host thought his wife should get a job and begin to work full time. The radio host told the man, "I guarantee that when your wife begins to work, unless you fix the problem, in time you will be worse off than you are now." The problem is overspending, and the host's point was that adding a second income will just become an excuse to spend more. The only way to solve the problem is to tame the overspending beast. Many people are not willing to change this reckless spending habit, and unless they do, they will always have financial problems.

Unfortunately, our government is not a good example. It habitually spends more than it takes in and it continually borrows and adds to an unimaginable deficit that threatens all of our futures. The government's remedy to its overspending problem is to tax more, print more money, and borrow more. Someday, we are headed for a crisis unless this reckless spending can be stopped, and this is true for us as families and individuals as well if we don't control our spending.

B. Keeping Up with the Joneses

As human beings we have an innate desire to be like those around us. This desire to have what others have is in our blood as well. In a former church where I served as pastor, a few young men had each purchased a particular type of car. There were several of these young men that hung around together and were great friends. I noticed that it wasn't very long before another young man in "the group" purchased the same kind of car, brand new, of course. I happened to know a bit about the young man's financial situation, how he was maxed out on his credit cards and very much in debt. But I understand that he wanted to be one of the guys. "If the guys all have boats, I got to have a boat." "If the guys have expensive home entertainment systems, I've got to have one . . ."

People are this way about their cell phones. What would people think about you if you didn't have a smart phone or had no phone at all? You wouldn't want your 12-year-old daughter having only a clunky old flip phone when all her friends have $1,000 smart phones that cost their parents $200 per month? Well, maybe it wouldn't bother you, but it would bother your daughter, and she would pressure you to exasperation until she got one. If our siblings have a nice whatever, often we want the same. We don't want to think that our siblings or in-laws have it better than we do. As we get older, we might not feel as much of a need to keep up with our friends or work associates (at least not consciously). But there is something about that brother-in-law having a nicer car than ours that fries us. As I mentioned, my father was death on new cars, and naturally insisted that I follow his example. I have only purchased two in my life. The second one I bought right after my brother-in-law just happened to buy his. Do you think there was any connection?

Financial Hero Number 3

I have a good friend who is convinced he does not have to have what everyone around him has. He has never been married, and although he has a driver's license, he does not have a car and never has had or wanted one. His mode of transportation is bicycle, which he rides every day regardless of weather. He estimates that he puts six or seven thousand miles on his bike yearly. After several years the bike completely wears out and he is forced to buy a new one. He has never owned a house and has never wanted one. He lives in a small one-bedroom apartment and he doesn't have a couch or a comfortable chair. There is only a card table, a couple of folding chairs, a bed, and a small dresser. He told me once that he wouldn't need a two bedroom apartment because he has plenty of room.

He doesn't have a cable TV bill because he doesn't have a television. He has no computer, although he did operate a computer on his job before he retired at age 55. He rarely goes out to eat and he rarely eats meat. He eats almost exclusively dried oats, raw fruits and raw vegetables. After a routine physical, his doctor told him, "I don't know what you're doing, but keep doing it." He is amazingly healthy and is very disciplined. Every morning at 4 or 5 a.m., he goes out on his bicycle for a 20-plus mile jaunt. He says he likes to see the sun come up. He does this every day, rain or shine and in all four seasons. Then, in the afternoon he takes another long ride. Presently, he tells me, he is on his bicycle about five hours a day. This will decrease when he can go back to his "retirement job" at the library, which is shut down, because of the COVID-19 virus.

On occasion he visits one of his three brothers, all of whom are medical doctors and reside in different parts of the country. When he visits them he rarely

Craig's bike riding friend, Richard

flies but takes a bus or train. He is by no means a tightwad, however. He gives generously to his church, to which he is very committed and where he serves as church treasurer. During the COVID-19 pandemic, the government gave out stimulus checks to most Americans.

Richard donated his entire check to an organization that provided food for the needy. This is his style. He is a giver. His passion is helping children to read. He has spent countless hours as a tutor and as a volunteer mentor to underprivileged adolescents. Richard has offered to pay the college tuition of one of the young men whom he is trying to persuade to extend his education. He is very devoted in his faith. He and I are polar opposites in terms of politics and in some theological issues, but we agree to disagree. I was shocked when he told me that he had recently purchased a smart phone. It was so out of character for him. My friend is not in danger of entering into the high-tech modern world, though. I told him about this incredible app that he could put on his phone and track his speed, his mileage, and elevation while he is on his bicycle. He got very quiet. That is his way of saying "no". But I only bring up my friend Richard because his lifestyle teaches us that it is possible to dance to the beat of our own drum. We do not have to have what everyone around us has. Few of us, however, have the courage to not conform to the lifestyles and thinking of those around us.

But I only bring up my friend Richard because his lifestyle teaches us that it is possible to dance to the beat of our own drum.

Richard is truly his own person. Inwardly, I wish that I, like Richard, could get rid of my car, my house, and three-fourths of my worldly possessions and just be content with a few clothes, a few pieces of furniture, and a very simple lifestyle. We have complicated our lives with too much property and stuff to maintain. The more we have, the more insurance we need, the more things break down, the more maintenance, the more record keeping. . . . It is a heavy burden. I admire someone like Richard who has refused to throw himself underneath the weight of it all. Even though he has very little, he seems extremely happy. Our society has convinced us that we have to keep purchasing an endless stream of material things in order to be content. It is not true, and Richard's lifestyle shows that we can be content, fulfilled, and happy with very little.

C. Not Being Teachable

There was a professional ball player whose name shall go unmentioned. The man had incredible power. When he would hit a homerun, the ball wouldn't fly out to the bleachers; it would shoot out like a rocket. It was jaw dropping to watch him when he connected. When this baseball player got hold of one, the announcer wouldn't say, "Hey, maybe this one has a chance." It was more like, "It's gone, goodbye!"

I once saw the homerun hero drop one hand accidentally as he swung at the ball. Well, the ball landed in the left field bleachers. "Oh my, this guy can hit homers swinging the bat with one hand!" people exclaimed. Before a game, I heard one of the announcers discussing this powerful hitter. "Yes he is good, but he could be great if it weren't for one problem. He refuses to listen to advice. The batting instructors make suggestions but he fails to listen." I'm afraid a lot of people are like this could-have-been-a Hall-of-Famer when it comes to their finances. They simply won't listen to any suggestions on how to invest, save, and budget. They don't want anyone telling them what to do. There are many people who have had good paying jobs but are now approaching their retirement years without a dime saved. Certainly they heard people tell them along the way, "You've got to start saving for retirement," but they wouldn't listen. There are people who are in dire financial straits after suddenly losing their jobs due to COVID-19. Some of them refused to listen to the wise voices of the past telling them, "You've got to have an emergency fund."

Years ago I knew a couple who, like many Americans, lived from paycheck to paycheck. After many years of not saving or investing or owning a home they were barely getting by, even though both had good paying jobs. I took a little risk during one time with them and suggested that they try budgeting, establishing a savings account, and not purchasing on credit. The woman said, "Oh, you sound just like my brother-in-law." Well, I knew her brother-in-law, who happened to be an accountant. He lived frugally and saved and spent responsibly. For whatever reason, the couple failed to listen to advice and have suffered needlessly for years.

Perhaps taking advice is something I come by naturally. I took the

Craig's mother, Wilma Burton

advice of my father when it came to managing money, but my mother was really the one who influenced my life dramatically with three important pieces of advice she offered me. First, she persuaded me to make Jesus Christ my Lord and Savior. I was not the least bit interested, even though she insisted that I go to church, Sunday School, and every Christian youth event in Wheaton, Illinois, where I grew up. Finally, at the age of 15, I gave in and I told God, "If you're up there you can have me." Things have not been the same since. That has been the most influential decision in my entire life, and if it hadn't been for my mother's influence, I could have gone a completely different and destructive route.

My mother was really the one who influenced my life dramatically with three important pieces of advice.

The second bit of advice had to do with the choice of my wife. When I was in high school, my mother worked with a woman whose teenage daughter attended my high school. "Why don't you ask Mary Benson out on a date?" Mom queried. Now, how many young men would take such a suggestion from his mother? "Sorry, Mom but I will decide who I ask out, thank you."

Craig's Wife Mary in High School

Not me. I figured no one on this earth had my interest more in mind than my own parents, so I asked Mary Benson out. Three years later we were married, and here is a tribute that I recently wrote about her on Facebook:

> Today I found myself thinking about as I often do of just how wonderfully blessed I am to have my wife Mary. We have been married for over 47 years. She was my high school sweetheart, the girl I took to the prom, the one I have been in love with since I was 17 years old. To me she is the human

example of what Jesus is like. She doesn't get angry and she is always kind and loving to others. Nothing in this world seems to upset her. I have told people that being married to her is like being married to a perfect person. She doesn't have glaring faults and doesn't have a dark side. Where I find myself struggling and getting upset over things, she seems to take everything in stride. Today, when I am pressured and stressed, I ask myself, "Now, how would Mary handle this?" I want to be like Mary because she is like Jesus. Everyone who has ever known her likes her. Her kindness and her smile bring warmth to all. I have never known a person who didn't like and admire her. We have been through some rocky roads together but she has prevailed and has never once wavered in her faith, setting an example for all. She was once very active and athletic, a high school and college athlete and coach. She loved to bike, hike, run, swim, play volley ball etc. Today, she struggles with great physical challenges. She can only walk just a little bit with the help of her walker. Getting herself dressed and taking showers are very hard for her. Standing for very long hurts her back. She can't make the bed and she can't clean the house. She is instructing me how to cook as she sits at the kitchen table. Without me Mary would have to be in a nursing home. Yet in all of this she never

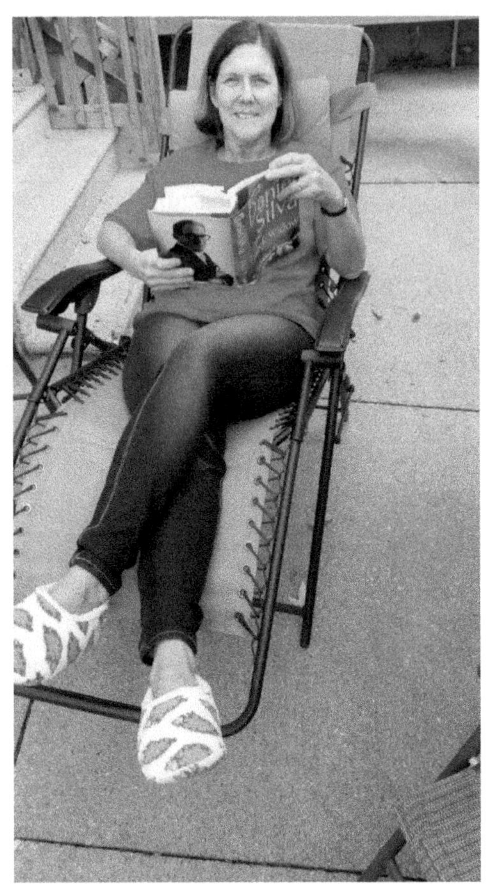

Craig's Wife Mary Burton

complains, is not discouraged, or depressed. She still remains cheerful and content, drawing even more closely to her Lord and Savior. Now, I'm not writing this because it our anniversary or because it is Mary's birthday. I am writing this on just an ordinary day as I'm thinking, as I often do, of how greatly blessed I am to be married to my wife, Mary.

The third treasure of advice that my mother gave me was in respect to my career. After college, I didn't know what I wanted to do with my life and I was frustrated. I had tried a few things but nothing seemed to be working out.

A Young Pastor Craig Burton

At my mother's strong suggestion, I went to speak to a friend of hers who happened to be the president of Northern Baptist Seminary in Lombard, Illinois. It was a half hour discussion that would change the course of my life. Within a few weeks, I was enrolled in seminary, working in a local church as a youth pastor, and at the start of a rewarding ministry career. Here were three pieces of advice from my mother that literally formed who I would become and am today.

I bring up all of this because many people are in terrible financial shape today. For some it is due to circumstances beyond their control but for others it is due to poor financial decisions and a simple lack of discipline. For many others, they are where they are because they just wouldn't listen to advice. If someone is willing to learn, there is a lot of information out there on retirement and personal financial management from reputable sources. I have read many books and articles on the subject. More importantly, there are people around us who are doing it right financially. Doesn't it seem like a wise thing to pick their brains on how they do what they do? Buy them lunch and ask questions. It might be the best piece of advice you have ever heard, well worth the price of the lunch. And by the way, be careful to whom you listen. You wouldn't ask a 400-pound person for his advice on how to lose weight. You wouldn't ask a person who is drowning in debt how to manage finances. Get advice from someone who is doing it right.

D. Illegal Drugs and Alcohol

More people have a problem with substance abuse than what you may think. For 18 years I was a pastor in a church in southern Iowa. Although the town was small, it had a big drug problem. Consequently, some townspeople and I started a local chapter of an international ministry called, "Addicts Victorious." We saw some great successes but many more tragedies and even deaths. Addictions like this, as we all know, ruin every aspect of a person's life, including their finances. One woman bought a brand new Ford Ranger truck that was confiscated by the authorities because she had illegal drugs in the vehicle. Another woman lost her entire farm, which was worth more than a million dollars because she was growing marijuana on it. Far worse, she eventually lost her life due to complications from alcohol abuse. The town was economically depressed and many were unemployed or underemployed. One man from the group had one of the better paying jobs in town in a particular plant that had a reputation for offering a higher hourly wage. The man had worked there for years and years and should have had a nice car and home. So I was shocked when I saw the old run-down trailer in the trashy trailer court where he lived. His car looked just as bad. Cocaine is an expensive habit, and most of the money he had made through the years had gone to support his drug cravings. The drug dealers that I knew over the years of co-leading the group were often broke or were living in ugly rat holes of homes. They would make a lot of money but they would spend even more on their habits. The addicts would lose jobs, homes, spouses, and would reap untold sorrow on their children. There is a big push to legalize marijuana today, but I wish you could have heard a particular woman from the group who weekly complained, "All that my husband wants to do is smoke pot and sit on the couch. He doesn't want to work. He doesn't want to be a father. He doesn't want to do anything. . . ." Need I say more?

E. Not Being Willing to Better Oneself

I am friends with a pastor from the African nation of Liberia. He tells me that in his congregation there is a 70 to 80 percent unemployment rate. There just isn't opportunity for someone to get a better job, further skills, or a higher wage. I'm not saying this to heap guilt upon anyone's situation, but the circumstances are far different in the United States. We live in the land of opportunity, but it is up to us to take advantage of the many resources we have available to us. For example, I know a young lady who became pregnant in high school. As it happens in many cases, the father wanted nothing to do with the baby or the young woman after the birth of their child. Many single moms in such situations would have conceded to a life of poverty. But this woman finished high school and then while raising her daughter went on to earn her bachelor's and master's degrees. Afterwards, she landed a good job working as a pharmacist. If you ask her, she would tell you that it was far from easy. It took sacrifice, hard work, and incredible dedication, but she did it. I fear too many feel that their financial situation is hopeless and fail to do everything they possibly can to better themselves.

A person called into a radio host on financial program. After he explained his financial situation, the host said, "You are right, you cannot possibly make it on your low salary. My advice to you is to do something to better your situation. Take classes, learn a new trade, or move to where you can find a better job. But let me stress that you have the responsibility to take care of your family, and you need to do everything you can to improve your situation so that you can."

There are two ways of looking at life when we're not making it financially. One is from the perspective of the victim. The other is from the perspective of choice. "I choose to do something, with God's help, to better myself so that my children and I will not have to live in poverty."

Government assistance is important, and it definitely has its place. But some people would rather get a small government check than work. Unfortunately, in some cases people are better off financially on public assistance than they would be working their low wage jobs that pay no benefits. Some people have refused to work because of this. Some families have been on assistance for generations. They know nothing else. The youth pastor, whom I worked with for years in my former church, told me that he would often have to try to convince some of the young people that they needed to shoot for something more than a lifetime of living on public assistance like their parents. They had no ambition to work or to shoot for a good paying job, because what they saw was parents, uncles and aunts, grand-parents living on welfare. It is a mindset that traps people from bettering themselves, and it is a road to poverty. And by the way, it is not just the lower classes that struggle with this mindset. Recently, I read an article in which during the pandemic, a business executive had somehow arranged for her employees to go back to work because she had established "safe distancing" and other precautions at the work place. She thought her workers would be thrilled. Instead she was shocked to hear that the far majority were very upset because they knew that they would make more on unemployment than they would on their jobs. Isn't there something wrong with this picture?

F. Not Being Willing to Give

The Bible says that if we tithe, God will pour out on us a blessing that we cannot contain (Malachi 3:10). Many people whom I have counseled with that have overspent also have failed to give. I remember one couple, both had good jobs, a beautiful home, and brand new vehicles, but they were broke. Not only were they overspending, they didn't give a dime to God's work. Both problems were the cause of their financial woes. A man from the congregation helped them set up a budget, devise a plan for paying off their debt, and instructed them to start tithing. It wasn't a quick fix because it can take years to undo a financial hole like they were in but they got started on the right track. I am convinced that my wife and I are substantially better off because of our consistent giving to God's work and to his people through the years. God has blessed me in ways that I could never have imagined and it is mostly because of how we have given. Giving is a source of joy as the next story indicates.

A wealthy man in a church where I served made a huge impact on my life. He had a home that looked like a mansion from my perspective. He drove expensive cars and seemed to indulge in an expensive lifestyle. Most of us have known wealthy people like this, or we have admired their homes on the other side of town or across the country. Because of my position at the church, I learned that this man gave a lot of money to various ministries. He would always do it anonymously and very few had any inkling of what the man was giving. He made a big contribution to the church building program, and he helped to support missions. But what impressed me was the way he was giving to church planting projects, which was where his heart was. He would buy a church building, and then he would pay for a pastor's salary until the church could get on its feet. There was five or six such church planning ventures that he was almost completely funding. People thought the district of our denomination was really zealously pursuing church planting. It was not the district. It was this man who was paying for everything. Remember what I said about receiving advice? If you find someone who is doing it right, sit down with them and find out what they are doing. That's exactly what I did, and this is what he told me: He said that he saved enough for him and his family to live the "good life", and he gave the rest away.

I had already seen his home, and I knew that his good life was beyond what I could imagine for myself. From my perspective, he was living like a king. So I asked him, "What you're telling me is that you give away 80 or 90 percent of what you make and live off the rest?" He said, "Yeah, something like that." I admitted to him that even though I was a minister I could never give that much away, no matter how much I made. He looked at me like he was totally surprised. "Why?" he replied. "Don't you realize the blessing you would be missing out on?"

These words were life changing to me. He had no idea how his example and what he said would change my life. I started to give more and at times generously. Later, there was a young missionary who visited the church. He told me privately that he wanted to raise financial support for his ministry but needed some audio-visual equipment so he could make worship presentations. He had no money, and I thought to myself, *My friend Don would just pay for the equipment. He wouldn't call a committee meeting or put the request on the prayer chain. He would just take out his checkbook and pay for it.*

So I told the young missionary, "You pick out what you want and I'll pay for it." The next week he came with a catalogue and he showed me a picture of the equipment and I made out a check for him. My friend was right. It was a blessing. I may have lost my reward because I just told you about what I never told anyone, but there is a tremendous blessing when we give generously and cheerfully. When we don't give, we not only hurt ourselves financially, we miss out on a tremendous blessing.

I also learned that there was a time when things were not so good for my generous friend. He had suddenly lost his job and with a wife and five children, the situation was not very cheerful. But my friend started his own business, and he began to make money hand over foot. Losing his job was the best thing that ever happened to him. But through it all he gave faithfully and generously, not just in terms of the amount but in the percentage of his giving. The more he gave the more God blessed him financially and spiritually as well. The man taught me that it is truly a good thing to give and to give generously.

My wife and I enjoy watching the television program "The 700 Club". Almost daily there is a special report featuring someone who was once in financial trouble financially. When they started to tithe or give ten percent of their earnings to God's work, their finances turned around. It didn't happen overnight but it happened. A lot of things have contributed to the financial success that I have enjoyed. I've talked about savings, establishing a budget, wise investing etc. If I had to identify the most important aspect of being able to retire comfortably, it would definitely be in the area of giving. Sometimes after reviewing my financial assets I will ask myself, "Where did all of this money come from?" I remind myself that I have earned very little over the years on a minister's salary. There is only one explanation. God has been faithful to us and has blessed our faithful and generous giving. I mentioned a verse from scripture before and I will repeat it because it is so important. "Bring the whole tithe into the storehouse, that there may be food in my house. Test me in this," says the LORD Almighty, "and see if I will not throw open the floodgates of heaven and pour out so much blessing that you will not have room enough for it" (Malachi 3:10). This is the only scripture in which we are told to actually test God. He says, "Test me and give like I've instructed you and I will give you a financial blessing that you won't be able to even contain." Many have tested God in terms of giving and they have found God faithful in turning their dyer financial situations around. If you are struggling financially, the main thing I would tell you is to give generously to God's work and the needy and someday you will also wonder, "Where did all this money come from." Giving according to God's instructions is by far the most important aspect of getting our finances in order and in being able to retire comfortably.

G. Loving to Shop

Someone suggested that men don't shop; they hunt. In other words, according to this theory, men generally go the store looking for a particular item as opposed to going from shop to shop or mall to mall seeing what is there. Call it window shopping or call it whatever you want, loving to shop can become an expensive hobby. Store owners want shoppers to go through their entire store so you will be tempted to buy more things than what you'd intended. Have you ever noticed how the milk is in the far back of the grocery store? They don't want you to just come in for milk; they want you to go through 12 different isles so that you will fill up your cart. You might not think you will pick up much when you go to the mall, just to browse. But it is amazing how instead of just looking, you end up buying that extra pair of shoes or outfit. While you're eyeing the cute sweaters, your husband is in the electronic section viewing that humongous TV screen, or he's in the lawn and garden center checking out the expensive John Deere riding mower. Loving to shop, even if you are just planning to look, can cause impulse buying and an accumulation of stuff you just don't need. Going to garage sales or to resale shops can also become destructive habits to get into. Although you might save money, you are going to accumulate things you just don't need.

A man in a former church where I was pastor loved to go to farm sales. He wouldn't miss a single one in the county, and he loved to pick up old farm machinery. Well, actually, he loved to pick up everything at theses sales and auctions. When he died, his family had to have a sale to try to get rid of all the stuff he had accumulated, and 90 percent of it he never even used. People do it because they love the thrill of buying and accumulating. I will go to resale shops and garage sales only when I'm looking for something in particular. But every time I go, I'm tempted to pick up something I don't need or even want. By the way, I learned that if you ever attend a farm auctions, never scratch your nose or rub your eye! I did it once as a young pastor and the auctioneer stopped the auction and asked me, "Are you bidding on this tractor, young man?" I quickly explained that I just had something in my eye and he went on with "Fifteen thousand, sixteen thousand, who'll give me seventeen?" It was a close one and I almost became a part-time farmer just because I scratched my nose.

Some people shop when they've had a bad day and they're a little depressed. I read of a woman who would go out and purchase a brand new pair of shoes every time she got down in the dumps. She must have been depressed a lot, because in her closet there were hundreds of pairs of shoes, most never worn. If you love to shop, find something else that you like to do instead. Take up pickle ball or bicycling, or maybe professional hog calling, or whatever.

H. Get-Rich Schemes

Proverbs 13:11 (NLT2) Wealth from get-rich-quick schemes quickly disappears; wealth from hard work grows over time.

Usually when someone tries to get rich quickly by betting a lot of money on a fast horse, it back-fires and they find themselves riding on the backside of a donkey. The old adage is correct, "If something sounds too good to be true, it probably is." When I was first married, my in-laws got involved in a pyramid soap-selling scheme. I attended one of the business meetings that were intended to fire up the people who had invested in the company. People would give testimonies of how selling these soap products had changed their entire lives. "I was a drug addict, and my wife and I were on the verge of divorce, but our lives were saved by 'Sudsy Sales'." I never knew that soap was the answer to everyone's problems! Well, like all pyramid businesses, the people at the top made money but the little guy at the bottom got nothing except a garage full of soap products he couldn't get rid of. The company eventually went out of business, but not before a lot of people had lost the money they invested by buying these products that nobody wanted to purchase.

I am skeptical of someone who has some investment they want me to sink a lot of money into, promising me great returns. Again, if it is too good to be true, it probably is. Remember Bernie Madoff? He was convicted of duping 4,800 clients out of 64.8 billion dollars. He used a classic Ponzi scheme to cheat his investors, many of whom lost their life savings. Clients who were taken in were offered higher returns than what traditional investments were making. Well-known reputable people could testify that they were actually getting these kinds of returns. That's how a Ponzi schemes works. The initial investors do make money, but that is only to lure other poor suckers into their scheme. In reality, there is no money behind the investments. The scammers simply rob Peter to pay Paul. Eventually they get caught, but not until they have destroyed the financial well-being of their victims.

A similar scam, called the "Foundation for New Era Philanthropy" raised $500 million from 1,100 donors and embezzled $135 million from 1989 until 1995. The man behind the plan, John G. Bennett, went after non-profit organizations, evangelical ministries, and colleges. When others heard that certain reputable organizations had invested in New Era and were receiving the promised returns, they thought the plan must be sound. It all goes to show that anyone can be taken in, and we have to be careful with whom we invest. The initial investors got good returns, but the later ones got nothing. If someone is promising investment returns that are way beyond what others are paying, run.

On his radio program, a certain Christian investor suggested that some ministers because they often don't make much money, will get involved in questionable investments that offer quick and high returns. They will intentionally get some of their parishioners to join them. The church members think, "Well it must be okay, because Pastor So-and-So has recommended it, and in fact he's invested in it himself." The radio host said he has seen some people who have lost a lot of money in such situations.

I knew a doctor who lost his entire retirement savings because he invested in a business venture that was introduced to him by a man in his church. The man who took him in was not a pastor, but he was a church leader and was well respected in the congregation. The doctor lost his nice nest egg right on the threshold of his retirement. The man offering the deal was well intentioned; he didn't mean to scam anyone, but he was involved in a really bad venture and he took others down with him.

Another recently retired woman lost two-thirds of her meager savings because she let a friend's husband, who claimed to be good with investments, handle her money. The sad lesson is just because someone is a friend or a respected individual doesn't qualify him or her to handle someone else's savings or retirement funds.

My view is that it is better to go with sound investments and reputable companies. You may earn fewer returns, but better to be safe than sorry. No scammer is going to be able to lure you through offering two to three percent returns; he or she will offer very large ones. "Hey, you want to triple your money?" Red flags should be raised when someone makes such claims. They can easily sucker someone who wants to take the fast track to getting wealth.

I. Helping Adult Children

I am not the only one who cautions against helping your adult children financially. I have read several articles advising against the practice. Doing so can not only put you in a financial bind but can cause your adult kids to become dependent on your pocketbook. Here are a couple of cases I am aware of:

Rex had been living in his parents' basement for many years. Years before, he lost his driver's license and didn't seem to have the wherewithal to get it back. Neither was he working or interested in working. This single man had it too good living off of mom and dad. At 38 years of age, don't you think it was time for Rex to be booted out of the nest? I have used the illustration many times during funeral services. I have said that heaven, according to the scriptures, is beyond our imagination, as it is written: "What no eye has seen, what no ear has heard, and what no human mind has conceived—the things God has prepared for those who love him" (1 Corinthians 2:9). Then I will say, "Now imagine your happiest moment ever; maybe it was your wedding day or the day you held your newborn baby. Maybe it was the day your 38-year-old son finally got a job and moved out of the house for the first time. Whatever it is, it can't hold a candle to what living in heaven with Jesus will be like." I have found that no matter how grief-stricken the funeral crowd is, the line about the 38-year-old son is guaranteed to get a hearty laugh.

But I have heard worse, a lot worse, about parents enabling their adult children. A 97-year-old woman complained to me about her son still living in her home. "He won't work, he won't move, and I can't sell the house with him still in it." "Well, how old is your son?" I couldn't help but ask. "Oh, he's seventy years old." Here's a man who never worried about saving for retirement, not as long he could take care of his mom's generosity and longevity. I didn't know if I should laugh or cry when I heard this story--seventy years old? As it turned out, the lady did sell the house from underneath her son. She moved out west to live with her daughter. I don't know what happened to her 70-year-old son. Maybe he found someone to adopt him.

There are emergency situations in which we need to help our adult children. Perhaps there is a divorce or an abuse situation. Maybe an adult child has serious medical issues. Of course I'm not against helping our adult children in such circumstances. But as a rule, when we get near or into our retirement years, we need to stop helping our kids. In fact, they should be helping us.

Children are to honor their parents, and one of the ways they can do this is by helping them with their senior expenses. I have witnessed some adult children who have done exactly this. For years, one man for paid for his parent's rent in an expensive retirement center. I believe God is pleased by this. I have known so many seniors who have been struggling financially while their adult children wouldn't offer them a dime. This shouldn't be. Yet I have seen too much of the other way around: seniors helping their adult children to the parent's harm. I have known seniors who have not been able to retire because they have helped their adult children purchase homes or cars. I know one lady who lost her house because of helping her son. "Well, Johnny had a drug problem and Johnny was in and out of jail. Johnny couldn't keep a job." I don't know exactly what the financial arrangements were but Johnny lost the home he was "renting to buy" from mom, and she ended up living in a subsidized apartment for the elderly. It is amazing how adult children with good paying jobs can become dependent on mom or grandma to fund their reckless spending. We can sadly enable our adult children through our giving. Let me say again, when we are retired or we are close to retirement, it is time for them to be helping us and not the other way around.

I have known so many seniors who have been struggling financially while their adult children wouldn't offer them a dime. This shouldn't be.

And now that I'm in my preaching mode, it is unconscionable how some adult children neglect their parents because they rarely call or visit. An older minister told me, "My kids insisted on me moving to the retirement center so that I could be near them. But now that I am here, I never see them and that includes the grandchildren." I have dealt with hundreds and hundreds of senior adults and their families. Many adult children and grand-child are wonderful in calling and visiting grandpa and or grandma, but there are many who simply neglect them. I addressed the issue through a special Sunday morning worship service where family members of our residents at the retirement center were invited to attend with their parents .The service was followed by a family church dinner. In my sermon I spoke tactfully about honoring our parents in their golden years by calling and visiting them regularly. Ephesians 6:2-

3 (NIV)[2] "Honor your father and mother"--which is the first commandment with a promise-- [3] "that it may go well with you and that you may enjoy long life on the earth."

It is hard for me to understand the type of neglect that I have witnessed. My father was in a nursing home for four years and I was 26 when he passed away. But during those four years I visited him every single day without fail. My mother died when I was 29 but for years, I called her every single day on the phone. If I wasn't visiting her, I was calling. Perhaps for this reason, it is difficult for me to see how some adult children rarely call or visit their parents. Maybe someone reading this will begin to take a greater interest in their senior parents and grandparents. Who cares if a person has their financial house in order and if they are on track for a good retirement? If he or she neglects the social, emotional and financial needs of their adult parents, it doesn't really matter does it? **1 Timothy 5:8 (NIV)** [8] If anyone does not provide for his relatives, and especially for his immediate family, he has denied the faith and is worse than an unbeliever.

J. Coming into a Lot of Money Quickly

My parents had both died by the time I was 29. They left a good (not huge) inheritance but stipulated that we would not be able to access the majority of it until we were 35. One of my two sisters was already beyond that age, and the other was just a couple of years shy of it. I couldn't understand why my dad made such a stipulation but now, looking back, I see the wisdom of his decision. He was concerned that in our youth we would foolishly spend our inheritance and go through it quickly. Proverbs 20:21 (NIV) says an inheritance quickly gained at the beginning will not be blessed at the end.

An article in "The Conversation" suggests that people in their 20s, 30s, and 40s who were given a large inheritance or financial gift quickly lost half the money through lavish spending or poor investments (Jay Zagorsky, "The Conversation: How Winning $1.54 Billion in Mega Millions Could Still Lead To Bankruptcy," January 12, 2016, October 24, 2018).

It is easy to be tempted to spend recklessly at any age when someone comes into a lot of money. When a person is younger, he or she may not have the wisdom to restrain. Those who are irresponsible with a small amount of money will probably be the same with a large sum.
Huntington Hartford lived from 1911 to 2008 and inherited $90 million dollars when he was only 12 years old. By today's standards his inheritance would be almost $1.3 billion. Huntington lost millions of dollars through poor investments in real estate and art, and he led an incredibly lavish lifestyle. He declared bankruptcy in 1992 and spent his final years living with his daughter as a recluse (Hess, Abigail CNBC, August 25, 2017)

I know a single man, although raised in a Christian home, was irresponsible in about every way imaginable as a young person and as an adult. Homelessness and drugs and reckless behavior were the norm for him. In his 50s he received a good inheritance when his parents died. It was too much for him to handle, however. He began to spend like money was going out of style. He took expensive vacations and bought cell phones and computers, cars, and much more. In six months he had gone through every dime, until finally he only had enough money for one day's stay in a motel. He was fortunate that a "Good Samaritan" relative allowed him to come into her home. The man, when asked what happened to all of his money, said, "Yeah, I blew it all, but I learned my lesson."

You learned your lesson? Do you think you'll ever receive an inheritance again? That was like shutting the barn door after the horses had already galloped out. "Whoever can be trusted with very little can also be trusted with much, and whoever is dishonest with very little will also be dishonest with much" (Luke 16:10).

"Whoever can be trusted with very little can also be trusted with much, and whoever is dishonest with very little will also be dishonest with much"

If we can't handle a little bit of money, how are we going to handle a lot? Some people think that if they would make more money, win the lottery, get an inheritance, all their problems will be solved. But if he or she were the kind of person who blew every dime they had while struggling, the same pattern would most likely follow after their ship comes in.

"So if you have not been trustworthy in handling worldly wealth, who will trust you with true riches?" (Luke 16:11). Jesus pointed out that if we are not responsible with money, we cannot be responsible with true spiritual riches. Our material things are just a test. We don't really own them. Everything we have belongs to God. We are stewards of his property. Good management of your money doesn't make you a saint. But if you can't handle money, you probably won't score too highly in the spiritual department either. This is not to say that all poor people or even the far majority of them have mismanaged their money. There are many who are destitute beyond any doing of their own. Some people live in countries where there are few opportunities to better oneself through education, higher paying jobs or through any jobs for that matter. Others are poor because of incurring medical bills they could not pay. On the other hand some people struggle financially because they have not been able to handle the great onslaught of money that has suddenly been thrust upon them.

People who come into a lot of money quickly often become irresponsible. They don't think that they have to work for or earn what they get. This is a serious condition. It is a welfare mentality of the wealthy. It would be just like giving children everything they ever wanted when they were young. They would think they never had to do chores or homework. How prepared would they be for the real world? Getting rich quickly can produce spoiled adults that have a difficult time adjusting to their new wealth. Worse, some people who come into money quickly make a total ruin of their lives and of the lives of others.

Jack Whittaker won $315 million in the US Powerball jackpot in 2002. Years later he said that he wished he would have torn up his winning lottery ticket. Thinking that his sudden-gained wealth would bring him ultimate happiness, he found that just the opposite occurred. He was the victim of thievery. A casino sued him for allegedly bouncing $1.5 million in checks. A woman claimed that he had groped her at a race track. His granddaughter used money he had given her to buy drugs, and she and her boyfriend died of overdoses. Jack's daughter died shortly afterward. Whittaker felt that all or most of the tragedies in this part of his life could have been avoided if he hadn't won the money. (Dahl, Melissa, nbcnews.com, "$550 Million Will Buy You a Lot of Misery", November 11, 2012)

A man by the name of William Post III was living on disability payments and had less than $3.00 in his bank account when he won $16.2 million in the Pennsylvania Lottery Jackpot. He immediately began to indulge in reckless spending. He bought a restaurant, an airplane, and an entire used car lot through impulse buying. His brother tried to murder him. His ex-wife hired a hit man to kill him so she could collect his money. His landlady conned him into giving her a third of his earnings. William Post III eventually filed for bankruptcy. "I was much happier when I was broke. Everyone dreams of winning money, but nobody realizes the nightmares that come out of the woodwork or the problems."

Post died broke at the age of 66. (O'Connor, Emma, Time "The Tragic Stories of the Lottery's Unluckiest Winners", May 20, 2013)

Other lottery winners have actually been murdered for their earnings, some by close family members. Jeffrey Dampier won $20 million in the Illinois Lottery in 1996. He was tied up and shot in the head by his sister-in-law and her boyfriend in 2005. (Weimar, Carrie, Tampa Bay Times, "Sentence: Life Times Three, June, 7, 2013)

Dr. Joseph Roncaioli, was a wealthy physician who made $20,000 per week in his gynecology practice in Ontario. His wealth didn't stop him from wanting more, however. In 1991 he won five million dollars in the lottery. After discovering that his wife had squandered his life savings and illegally signed documents that transferred all the lottery winnings to her, he murdered her in their Ontario mansion. High levels of drugs were found in her system and needle marks on her body. The doctor was found guilty of manslaughter and sentenced to prison. (Kari, Shannon, National Post, February 25, 2017)

Urooj Khan, was so addicted to buying lottery tickets, he swore off purchasing them at one point. After a period of abstinence, he decided to buy one more through which he won $1 million. Shortly afterwards he died of what was thought to be natural causes. A relative of Khan's grew suspicious, however, and insisted on a second autopsy. The results showed poisoning. Kahn's brother believes the lottery winner's wife put poison in his curry dish but no convictions were ever made in the man's murder. The case remains unsolved. (Gorner, Jeremy, Chicago Tribune, July 25, 2017)

.

One person said, "If you play the Lottery, good luck. If you win the lottery, you'll need even better luck." Lottery winners are constantly on the hunt from people wanting their money. One woman tells how perfect strangers would stop by her home asking for large sums of money. "For some reason," the woman complained, "everyone seems to need fifty-thousand dollars." Friends and family members expect financial favors, and lottery winners discover that no one seems to care about them. The temptation to spend recklessly and endlessly leaves many lottery winners broke, bored, or dead. Some winners have actually committed suicide. Many winners regret ever having purchased their winning lottery tickets.

The temptation to spend recklessly and endlessly leaves many lottery winners broke, bored, or dead.

I have never played the lottery for two reasons: First, I believe that doing so comes out of a desire to get rich. As mentioned previously, the love of money and a desire for riches brings people into all kinds of ruin. " People who want to get rich fall into temptation and a trap and into many foolish and harmful desires that plunge them into ruin and destruction. For the love of money is a root of all kinds of evil. Some people, eager for money, have wandered from the faith and pierced themselves with many griefs." (1 Timothy 6:9-10)

People who play the lottery generally have a desire to get rich quickly. This is a dangerous and wrong desire that has been the ruin of many. A lot of people are in prison today because of their love of money. They have sold drugs in order to get wealthy, or they have stolen and robbed. White-collar criminals are most often in prison because of their love of money, which has caused them to embezzle funds. I have dealt with two people in my past who have been sent to prison for embezzling money from the banks they worked at. One person told me, after he had been released from prison, that he was in the loan department at his local bank, processing loans for people borrowing money to buy cars and boats. The man said he got to thinking, "Why shouldn't I have a new car? Why shouldn't I have a new boat?" He went ahead and got those things by taking money from the bank. He eventually was caught and spent several years incarcerated at the state prison.

The second person I knew who stole money from a bank was a trusted bank employee of many years. She said that she embezzled the funds to help out her employer and bank owner who was in personal financial trouble. Really? Well, her so-called benevolent act sent her to prison and her boss nearly lost his bank. He said the bank wouldn't have been in trouble if she hadn't embezzled the funds. Both of these individuals who stole from their banks claimed to be Christians, but they had one glaring weakness: They loved money and wanted to get rich. Truly, the love of money is a root of all kinds of evil.

There are also examples of people whose love for wealth didn't cause them to steal from a bank, but rather from churches and Christian organizations. One man in a small community where I served as a pastor for 18 years stole money from his church (fortunately not mine) and several non-profit organizations where he volunteered as treasurer. His theft nearly ruined all the organizations at which he volunteered. Then there was a former administrator at the retirement center where I served as chaplain for 10 years. Supposedly a Christian man, the administrator embezzled thousands and thousands of dollars from the organization. The board at the time decided to not press charges in order to preserve the center's reputation in the community. Many years later, the retirement center still has not recovered financially from the former administrator's embezzlement.

If you love to play the lottery, you have not done anything

criminal. But you do desire to be rich like those who steal, cheat, and embezzle. It is all the same root of evil. There's nothing wrong with wanting to make a decent living and to provide for one's family. But the desire to get rich is destructive and ends in ruin. The ones committing crimes are the state and local governments who run the lotteries and encourage people to throw their money away. Some people who barely have enough to live on, always somehow find a way to play the lottery. The Journal for Gambling Studies suggests that people in the lower third income level spend the most on lottery tickets. They spend twice as much as those in the upper third income level. So basically the government is encouraging those who can least afford it, to throw away their money in their own state and federal sponsored gambling programs (Isidore, Chris "Who Is Buying Powerball and Mega Millions tickets?" CNN Money, January 6, 2018, 10:26 a.m. ET)

The second reason I don't play the lottery is because the odds of actually winning are so poor.
In 2016, the U.S. Powerball Lottery reached 1.5 billion dollars. The odds of winning were one in 292 million. A person would be 250 times more likely to be hit by lightning than to win. Those aren't very good odds; it's practically like flushing money down the toilet. Yet it is estimated that at least 90 million Americans play the lottery regularly ever year. When you tell someone how ridiculously low the odds of winning are, he or she will likely say, "Yeah, but someone has to win." That is true; but for every one winner there are millions and millions of suckers who have thrown away good money that could have been used for something needful.

The odds of winning were one in 292 million. A person would be 250 times more likely to be hit by lightning than to win.

Some time ago at a men's group, I shared my feelings on playing the lottery and the extreme low odds of winning. One man got quite upset with me. He told the group how his daughter purchased one ticket at a gas station and won a million dollars. He said it was the only lottery ticket she had ever purchased. So what do we conclude from this? Should we all go out and play the lottery because someone we know actually won? Yes, there are people that win. Nobody is disputing this. What I'm saying is that the odds for actually winning are so low a person would be far better going out to eat or putting money toward their electric bill. At least they would be using it for something practical instead of throwing it away. Remember, this book is not about how to get rich. It is about preparing for retirement through living well, within one's means. It includes being content with what we have, living the simple life. It is about not needing to have more, but being happy with making a reasonable living and having a budget that works. It is about entering into retirement not wealthy, but wealthy enough to be able to live off what you have saved and invested. Books about getting rich are a dime a dozen. This isn't one of them. It is about the little guy doing the right thing over a long period of time. It means you are not trying to make a killing but through living well, within your means, you will be able to be "sitting pretty" when it's time to retire.

K. Gambling

I've already spoken quite a bit about the lottery, but a lot of people who play the lottery don't gamble in other ways. My hunch, however, is that all gamblers play the lottery. It is just too much temptation for them. But there are a lot of other ways to gamble without playing the lottery. For example, betting on sports is huge today, and it has become very easy to do it through the internet. The government continues to relax standards on casinos and other types of gambling establishments. As it does, more and more people go through their savings and ruin their lives financially and in other ways. In a former community where I lived, a woman inherited a beautiful historic home and well over a million dollars. She lost all of it in just a few years because of gambling. Another woman in her seventies lost her home and her savings by betting regularly at the local casino. Although at one point she contacted the casino and other places she patronized and begged them not to let her into their establishments, she still found a way to gamble away all her money. Like with many people, for her gambling was a disease. When I knew her she had gone out of retirement to work as a waitress. It wasn't because she wanted to work. She should have had a comfortable retirement, but at that time she was working for minimum wage, trying to put food on her table.

I had one brief encounter with gambling when I was newly married. The lesson I learned was painful but it cured me for a lifetime. A little drive-by night carnival was set up just blocks from where my young bride and I were living. We strolled to the park one evening and walked past some of the gambling booths. A man lured me to his tent by flashing a nice little TV set before my eyes. "All you have to do, the man explained, "is play this simple game and you can win this TV."

My eyes got big. It seemed so easy. "I can do it!" I put my dollar down and even though I didn't win, I could try again for another dollar. *Two dollars isn't bad for a brand new TV,* I thought, so I put in another dollar and another. Before I realized what had happened, I had blown $20 in about three minutes. That was a lot of money back in those days. Twenty dollars was grocery money, and it hurt to lose it. I walked away without the TV and my wife and I both felt sick. But it was the best lesson I ever learned for $20. I told myself I would never gamble again and I never have.

Gambling grows from the same ugly root as playing the lottery. It is based on the love of money and a desire to get rich. As I have stated, both of these are a deadly combination.

A former parishioner who gambled a lot told me that most of the money he made came from gambling and not his regular job. He made his money from playing poker, and he was really good at it. He "knew when to hold them and when to fold them." In one year he made $100,000 playing poker. I asked him, how he would feel if he took a young man's entire paycheck in a card game. He said basically, "That's his problem. He knew what he was doing when he agreed to play, so it's just his tough luck." Well, this just didn't sit right with me. Although, I tried to convince my parishioner about the dangers of gambling, he continued to play.

I know a lot of Christian people who support the local casino not through gambling but through eating at their restaurant. They have great food, I'm told. Casinos offer their food at great prices to lure you to their slot machines or whatever they get you to gamble with today. Even though the odds are heavily stacked against the gambler, like the lottery player, the gambler at the casino is convinced that he can beat the house and win. If that were true, would the casino even exist? Just think of their elaborate buildings that sprawl out several acres, and the hundreds of people they employ, not to mention their race tracks. Would they have all of this if gamblers were winning? The house "holds all the cards" and only fools think they can beat the odds. You might win some, but you will lose a lot more. While working out at a local gym, I met a man who told me that he won $10,000 at the local casino. He said it was the only time he ever gambled and he used the money to pay off his truck. He said he would never gamble again. I'll bet you 10 to one that the man will go back to the casino. Sorry, I mean to say that it's *very likely* he will go back to the casino!

I compare myself to the tortoise in the story about the tortoise and the hare. Some people are like the hare. They're on the fast track, buying, spending, moving quickly, and it may work for them. I am not knocking them. But let me suggest that the slow and steady saver and investor, the tortoise, the steady plodder is more likely to win the race to retirement. I am not rich and have had no desire to do anything but live a simple life well. When it came time to retire, I was ready financially. I was not rich but I could live comfortably off my reasonable retirement nest egg and my Social Security. By keeping my living expenses low, I could carry on in my retirement years as I always have, living well, within my means.

My brother-in-law speaks of his father, who managed his money in a way I admire. He never made much money, working as a maintenance man and carpenter for a local private school. He worked in the same job for most of his employment years and lived in the same modest home. My brother-in-law told me his father often said that he never saw a dime that wasn't worth saving. He tells how his father, through salvaging from here and there, built an entire bathroom in his home for $300. He owned cars that he drove for many years because he took care of them. He saved enough money to send all three of his children to college. When it came time to retire he wasn't rich but he had plenty to support his conservative lifestyle until he died. He also gave generously to his church and to God's work. When I announced my retirement and explained a bit of my conservative financial philosophy to my brother-in-law, he said "Craig, you're just like my dad." Yes, it is true. That is who I am and who I want to be: the little guy, a plodder, saver, conservative investor, generous giver--who is sitting pretty at retirement.

Like the tortoise, I have done the right conservative things over a long period of time and now entering into retirement, I am "sitting pretty" because I have learned to live well, within my means. I trust this picture of living conservatively, plodding along slowly but surely, being content with what you have and being able to be secure at retirement will resonate within you. I am living a lifestyle and suggest that you follow my example of not zipping around like the hare, spending, accumulating nicer and newer, living from paycheck to paycheck, but rather, taking the financial race slowly and determinedly. You may find in your deliberate pace that you will get to the retirement finish line before and in better shape than the hare.

I enjoy sports. I was raised in the Chicago area and I enjoy the Bears and the Cubs, but I try to look the other way when I hear of the outrageous salaries that many of the athletes are making today. In 2016 the average annual income for a US household was $57, 617, but the average income for professional athletes was somewhere between two to 6.5 million. Some professional athletes make far more than this. In 2019, three NBA athletes signed contracts ensuring them $40 million per season. It always seemed funny to me when I hear of an athlete making $20 million a year, holding out for more money or going to another team who will pay him even more. He tells reporters, "Well, I have to take care of my family." Take care of your family! How much does your family eat, for crying out loud? (De Piccioloto, Elad "Do Professional Athletes Deserve Their Inflated Salaries?" Perspective Media LTD, 2017, July 13, 9:00 a.m.)

While I don't feel comfortable with athletes making such huge salaries, there is certainly nothing morally wrong with it. A person should be able to make as much as he or she can. John Wesley, father of Methodism, said, "Make as much as you can, save as much as you can, give as much as you can." Sounds good to me, but I only bring up the issue of athletes' huge salaries to demonstrate how obtaining large sums of money can be ruinous to some people. Where some athletes who have made large salaries have done well, others have come to tragic ends.

Tony Owusu identified five well-known professional athletes who filed for bankruptcy after they retired from their sports. The athletes, whom I won't mention by name, each had career earnings between 55 to 400 million dollars. Owusu also quoted from a 2009 Sports Illustrated issue that as many as 78 percent of professional NFL players file for bankruptcy or have great financial struggles after retiring from their sports (Tony Owusu, "5 Athletes Who Went Broke After Retirement, and How You Can Avoid Doing This," The Street, April 11, 2018, 3:22 p.m., EDT).

That's the fast track, the hare way of spending. It is giving no thought to the future but rather focuses on living and spending extravagantly now. Granted these athletes face all kinds of pressures that influence them to spend recklessly, but still they represent the opposite of how we want to live. We don't want to attempt to make ridiculous amounts of money quickly and spend it stupidly. That's the lifestyle of the hare, and I don't know how to even begin to tame such a wild beast. But you and I are going for the tortoise approach. We're not flashy in our slow and steady financial racing, but in the end we will get there "sitting pretty".

L. Remortgaging Your Home

I would never say never, but usually people who remortgage their home have a really difficult time repaying their debt. If people are struggling financially, taking on more debt, especially while endangering their home, will usually only exacerbate the problem. If the trouble is overspending, taking on more debt will in time just make things worse. I would not take out a mortgage on a home to remodel the kitchen or to enlarge the garage. This indicates a possible money management danger. If someone remortgages their home to pay medical expenses or because of extended unemployment, that is another thing, but to me, taking out a second mortgage should be avoided as much as possible.

M. Borrowing from Your 401(k)

The same principle goes for borrowing from one's retirement funds. At age 59 and a half, a person can do it without penalty. But even then he or she will have to pay taxes on the extra income. The worst thing is that it is just too tempting to not pay the money back. It's a sacrifice to save for retirement, but it is well worth it. Thirty years away seems like a long time to save for something when you're young, but someday those years will have passed. Don't be one of the people who come up short when the day does finally surface.

Borrowing from your retirement is something I just wouldn't do. It is simply too risky. Get a part-time job, and if you absolutely have to, borrow, but I wouldn't do it from my retirement funds. During the days of the corona virus, the government has made special provision for people to borrow penalty-free from their retirement funds. I think it would be better to take out a low-interest loan, even on a credit card, if need be. If a person has a good emergency fund and is living well, within that individual's means, there shouldn't be too many scenarios that would necessitate borrowing from a 401(k).

N. Expensive Collections and Hobbies

Having minimalist tendencies, I am not real fond of collecting a bunch of stuff that will clutter up my house. I had a mass of trophies for running races that I had collected over the years. One day I looked at it all and asked myself, "Why do I want to dust all this stuff?" So I threw it all out. Nobody cared about it anyway; it was just plain junk. If you want to collect stuff and clutter up your house, that's your business. For the purposes of this book, my objection is the cost. I have known people who can hardly pay their bills and who live paycheck to paycheck because they insist on funding their expensive collections and hobbies. I knew a man who collected and restored antique cars. They were expensive, and although he made a good salary, he couldn't afford them. His wife complained that whenever he got money, he would use it to buy a new engine for one of the Fords he was restoring in the backyard.

Another man told me that he and his wife lost thousands of dollars through collecting antiques. The reason was because, when the internet came into being, regular antiques were not as rare as once thought. You may have believed you had the only antique dresser of its kind, but when sites like eBay began you could get on the internet and find dozens just like the one you thought was so rare. The man said the coming of the internet dropped the price of his antiques and he lost a lot in the process. So my advice is if you have to collect, go for it. But if it keeps you from living well, within your means, saving, and preparing for a good retirement, you had better rethink what you are doing.

O. Traveling

I don't have many regrets in life, but one I do have is that I haven't been able to travel extensively like some other people have. Yet I know people who have spent so much money on travel and vacations, they have jeopardized their ability to retire. When I started working with retirees as a chaplain, some of the residents told me, "Chaplain, travel while you still can." I took their advice, and my wife and I took a nice cruise. We took a trip to San Diego and several trips to Florida. I'm glad we did, because today my wife's health has made traveling a lot more difficult. I wish we would have traveled more, but I would rather be able to retire than to have a lot of happy vacation memories. If you can travel, go for it, but don't compromise your retirement future to be able to do it. I have family members who write books and speak in public quite often. Many of their vacations have been paid for. That is a great way to go. I have a good friend who is a seminary professor, and he is flown all over the world to teach short-term in Bible colleges and universities. They don't pay him for his teaching, but they pay for his travel. He has taught in Romania and Vietnam many times. I am envious that I haven't had the opportunities some have had.

In the little traveling I have done, I have found ways to travel cheaply. I have stayed at the homes of relatives and friends. I have stayed at vacation places that have had special rates for pastors and Christian workers. I have borrowed friends' timeshares. But I would never own one. I became suspicious of them when a perfect stranger at a vacation spot offered to give me his. I was more suspicious when I realized that there are attorneys and websites that specialize in helping people get out of their timeshares. Thousands of people are stuck with them and can't get out of their monthly fees. I have friends that have timeshares and love them, but I see red flags and would never purchase one. There are inexpensive alternatives to taking vacations. The internet has a lot of potential places where you can go, entire homes you can rent, without getting harnessed with a lifetime monthly fee. I have also been to vacation sites where they would give you free housing, meals, and shows if you would only sit through their timeshare presentation. That was a mistake. The presentation was like mental torture. They insist on you buying into a timeshare and after you have repeated the word *No* fifty times, they bring in the manager and then his manager and finally the whole team tries to pressure you into signing. I should have been skeptical when I saw the single light bulb hanging from the chord tied to the ceiling, and the pitcher of water with a single glass on the table. ("Sure seems hot in here.") They stared me down under the lights and accused me of lying. "I thought you said that you do enjoy nice vacations, so why won't you sign? You're lying, aren't you?" Then they accused me of not loving my family. "A good family man would buy a dozen of these time shares. What's the matter with you?" I never have been a POW, but I sure gained sympathy for those who were after enduring the interrogation. Finally, they left with disgusted looks on their faces. I remember that look. It was the same look the teachers gave me when they saw me sitting in the principal's office when I was in sixth grade. It was not a look that boosted my self-esteem. So my interrogators finally gave up. They didn't even make me drink the whole pitcher of water. "You can leave now, and pick up your tickets for your free housing and meals at the front desk." I was emotionally beaten but I had not given in. They just didn't know how frugal I am! They had never met someone on my level before. Remember, there is cheap, there is cheaper and beneath both of those, there is Craig. I held my ground but I was wounded from the experience. I never knew that a person could get PTSD from listening to a timeshare presentation. Now, you would think that any normal person who had endured such a mental beating would never submit himself to such an experience again. That's exactly what I thought. "I will never accept such abuse again. I will sleep in my car. I will tent in my backyard, but I will never, under any circumstance, endure another timeshare presentation. I don't care what they offer me." But wouldn't you know it, five years later I did it again. It took me that long to recover from the previous sales presentation but I did it again five years later. I just couldn't turn down the free lodging, meals, and shows. After all, "free" is my middle name. I just couldn't resist. So I did it again, and it was worse than I remembered the first time. Still, I survived. Maybe it is kind of like going through labor. "I'll never do this again. Where is that ### who did this to me?" Sure enough, she forgets and a year or two later she's back in the delivery room. I'm just glad I'm not female. I probably would have had a dozen children.

P. Medical Expenses

One of the greatest threats to one's financial security is the high cost of medical care in our country. While studies vary in terms of their findings, one in particular claimed that 62.1 percent of bankruptcies are caused from people not being able to pay their medical bills. (Himmelstein, David U., MD, et al, "Medical

Bankruptcy in the United States, 2007: Results of a National Study," American Journal of Medicine Clinical Research Study, Volume 122, Issue 8, August 01, 2009, page 741). Another study claims that over two million people were adversely affected by medical expenses that they could not afford to pay. A woman who had breast cancer, told how she was unable to pay her medical bills that totaled $52,000. Even though she had insurance and paid her co-pay, she just couldn't afford to pay her medical bills. She had no choice but to file for bankruptcy. Further medical treatments, which included medications, additional surgeries and medical supplies forced her to consider filing for bankruptcy a second time. (Michael Sainato, "'I live on the street now': how Americans fall into medical bankruptcy," The Guardian, Thursday, November 14, 2019). This woman is not alone. It is estimated that as many as 530,000 people a year file for bankruptcy because of medical bills. The sad thing is that we can do everything correctly including, budgeting, saving, living within our means, and still face financial ruin because the cost of medical care is so outrageously high in the United States. This is one of the major reasons many people from our country are choosing to retire in nations that have a much lower cost of living, including the cost of medical care. On the plane while flying to California, I spoke to a man who said he would walk from San Diego to Tijuana, Mexico to get tooth implants. He said the cost was dramatically cheaper than having the work done in the States and that the quality was just as good. Some years ago, I researched extensively retiring in places like Ecuador, Panama, and Akiki, Mexico, near beautiful Lake Chapala. People of Akiki and the surrounding area enjoy a year-round climate similar to San Diego. The area has the largest number of Xpats from the United States and Canada. The cost of living is a fraction of what it costs to live in the States. Many people claim that they can live there just on their Social Security. Guadalajara, just 45 minutes away, boasts world-class medical facilities. One man wrote about getting knee surgery in

Guadalajara. It cost him $1,500. The same surgery in the United States would have cost him about $45,000. One Xpat said that moving out of the country forced him to give up some things, but at least he didn't have to worry about going under financially because of medical expenses. My first choice, if I were going to move out of the country would have been to the Lake Chapala area. I could envision myself renting cheaply a nice hacienda that came with a gardener and a housekeeper. I know, however, that deep in my heart I would miss the United States. I am an American down deep, tried and true. I also felt vulnerable because I don't know Spanish and don't understand the culture. These things are difficult to adapt to at my age. Lastly, my wife's health concerns made it too challenging to attempt such a drastic move. Through my research, however, I discovered that there are a lot more affordable places to live than the United States. I'm not talking about third-world countries and living in a grass hut. There are some places that boast high standards of living at a fraction of the huge cost that it takes to live in the States. The truth is that if a person is healthy and if he or she plans wisely, it is possible to be "sitting pretty" when it's time to retire. But if someone is not healthy, there is no sense of financial security in the United States. The high costs of medical care in our country can break anyone.

Q. Long-Term Health Care

Worse than the costs of medical care are the outrageous costs of long-term health care. At least if a person has good insurance, a large percentage of their medical costs can be deferred. But woe to the person who needs long-term health care. Again, there is no financial mercy for anyone who is in or who has a family member in this predicament. My father was in a nursing home in the late 1970s. To keep him there, it cost my mother $700 a month, which she paid for out of pocket. We thought the cost was outlandish. How could anyone pay $700 a month for nursing home care? Well, that was a drop in the bucket compared to what it is today.

Monthly nursing home costs in our country are seven or eight thousand dollars, and some are even more. (Average cost of private room nursing home care in the U.S. was $8365 per month in July, 2020). Can you afford an extra $8000 a month in your retirement budget? Some can, but most of us can't even imagine it. The alternatives are to pay out of pocket like my mother did or to go on government assistance. If your spouse goes into a long-term facility, they will let you keep your home and your car, but your spouse's assets go down to nothing. They will take his or her Social Security and pension, if he or she has one. So when it comes to retirement planning, you need to ask yourself, "Can I afford to live on half of my assets?" Nursing homes can't make it if all of their residents are on government assistance. It costs more to provide for a resident than what the government pays in many states. So long-term facilities are looking for a large number of private pay residents so their establishments can survive. Government reimbursement of nursing home costs varies from state to state. Long-term health care along with the high costs of medical care in our country will jeopardize anyone's retirement nest egg. Even if you have done everything right in your planning over the years, these costs can ruin a person financially. Assisted living is also very expensive. I know people who are paying up to $5,500 per month for this care. Although the average cost for assisted living care is $4,000 as of 2019, extra services are added on, and they are expensive. Help with one's medication can cost an extra $400 a month in certain facilities, as well as the cost of doing personal laundry. If someone needs help with getting dressed or with showering, it is all extra. Keep in mind the costs of rent, and services in nursing homes and assisted living increase usually on a yearly basis. Unfortunately, I have no answer for preserving wealth when a person is faced with the terribly high costs of long-term health care. Some people get long-term health care insurance. That is less expensive to get when a person is younger, but of course the younger you are, the longer you will pay your premiums. Some of the policies only cover two years of care and none that I am aware of pay for all a person's expenses. I know some individuals who receive financial assistance because of their military service. At least in the facility I worked for people could only apply for the assistance after they became residents. So they may or may not receive the financial help, and they wouldn't know until after they applied and moved in as a resident. The cost of long-term health insurance is expensive, and it is more expensive if you or your spouse has health issues. In our case, my wife couldn't even get the insurance because of her preexisting health needs. Some insurance companies no longer offer this particular type of insurance because of the escalating costs of health care and because people are living longer.

The cost of long-term health insurance is expensive, and it is more expensive if you or your spouse has health issues.

Another alternative to paying for long-term health insurance is to get an annuity with a long-term health care rider. Like all riders on annuities, it will reduce your monthly earnings payment and usually these policies only will cover a brief period of time and a fraction of what your monthly costs will actually be.

After nixing the long-term health insurance option and the annuity option, I decided to go with a home health care policy. For about $500 a year (the premium goes up yearly) I can receive limited home health care services for my wife. The services only last for a few months, but that would be a huge help in my estimation. Medicare also covers some home health care services, but there are greater restrictions and limitations.

The last thing I would recommend is making an appointment with an attorney or two who specialize in elderly care. They can give you advice and help protect some of your assets. I know of two in our community and one is quite a bit more expensive than the other, so shop around. Besides this, I would recommend doing all you can do to stay healthy. Eat right, exercise, lower your stress level, and pray that the Lord will give you good health. It is estimated that as much as 52 percent of Americans over the age of 65 will need to be in a long-term health care facility. If that isn't depressing, I don't know what is. Well, actually there is something more depressing, and that is the quality of care that a person actually receives in a long-term facility. I'm talking about: 1) How long does it take for a worker to actually answer the call light in each room? 2) How often are the nursing shifts short staffed? Estimates suggest from 70 to 90 percent of nursing homes are regularly short staffed. How well do you think your relative will be taken care of under such conditions? 3) How competent are the workers in the health-care facility where your relative is? 4) How loving and caring are the workers to the residents when no one is watching?

One thing to note is that there are a huge number of facilitics that are springing up to serve the aging Baby Boomer population. This has brought a shortage of qualified workers, not only in nursing homes but in some hospitals. The quality of care can do nothing but suffer. There are only so many patients that a nurse or CNA can attend to. A shocking book by Charlotte Digregorio, entitled *Everything You Need to Know About Nursing Homes* (Civetta Press, Portland OR, 2005) tells of the author's nightmare of having her mother in long-term health care facilities. Digregorio said that she had to constantly hound the staff to ensure that her mother was getting good care. Dissatisfied with the care that her mother was receiving, she moved her to another nursing home. She soon discovered that the care was just as bad there. Digregorio claims the problems of poor care are inherent to the long-term health care system in our country in general. In other words, she says that they are all bad no matter what they cost or how nice the facilities are. She ended up caring for her mother in her home.

Atul Gawande is a medical doctor whose father, also a medical doctor, was from India. In his book he writes of his father's amazement at how poorly the elderly are treated in the United States. In India, families care for their own elderly (Gawande, Atul , *Being Mortal: Medicine and What Matters in the End* New York: Picador 2014). They do not put them in nursing homes. One of Gawande's complaints is that American families neglect the emotional needs of our elderly parents. We want dad to be safe, so we take him from his home, take away his car, and stick him in an assisted living facility where he doesn't know anyone and is bored and depressed because he misses his tools and fiddling around in his garage. The adult children say, "Well, dad was falling and we wanted him to be safe." He may be safe, but now he's depressed because he misses his home and he doesn't have anything to do. We have made him safe but we have robbed him of what is most important to him. I saw it many times at the retirement center where I worked. One man in particular had an acreage where he loved to cut his grass, and trim trees. He had a huge garage where he loved to work on his lawnmower and tinker on little projects. The family thought that grandpa was too old for this kind of activity, and they wanted him to be safe. So they sold his home and moved him into a one-bedroom apartment. His adjustment was not a good one. Harvey never used to watch TV during the day. Now it is about all he does. I drove by recently and saw him sitting on a facility park bench, just staring into space. I thought, "*What have they done to that poor man?*" He may be safe but he isn't too happy.

Gawande's point is well taken. Some neighbors down the street are from India, and they told me that they have their elderly father and mother living in their home. They want to buy another house on their block where a brother would stay with the parents. They told me exactly what Gawande wrote in his book: "In India, we don't put our parents in nursing homes." It used to be the same way in our country. But now, with extended families living thousands of miles away and for economic and sometimes selfish reasons, we put our elderly in places you and I would never want to live. Maybe we need to rethink some of the way we care for our elderly and our dependence on long-term health care facilities that are questionable in their quality of care.

Long term health care is an expense that will derail most people's financial situations. Here is the question I'm raising: "Do you really want to go there anyway?" I, for one, do not. I will do whatever I can to keep my wife and myself out of one.

R. A Lack of Discipline

Planning and saving for a successful retirement takes hard work and consistency. It is easier to use the money we could be putting away for retirement for other things. There are times in my life when it really hurt to put the money into my IRA when I faced the financial pressures of raising a family. Especially when retirement was 30 years away or more putting money away for retirement seemed like a foolish use of money that I and my family needed then. We didn't go without the necessities like food and clothing but we did sacrifice in terms of sometimes going out to eat or on taking nice vacations because of my determination to save for retirement. It was a hard and painful sacrifice especially when the children were home and my wife was unable to work because of her home responsibilities. But looking back it was well worth the discipline involved that it took to save for a successful retirement. There are a lot of people who have made huge salaries through their working years but have little or nothing saved for retirement. One of the most common reasons for this is a lack of discipline. If you are a younger reader get in the habit of saving for retirement now. The earlier you start the better off you will be. As I mentioned earlier I am thankful for the employer who immediately started taking money out of my check when I was just 31 years old. They never asked me they just did it and I am glad now they did because they got me started saving for retirement at a relatively young age and they got me into a good habit. If you lack the discipline to save for retirement, let me offer a couple of suggestions: First, see if your employer will take money out of your check before you receive it. You will get so you will never miss it. Second, remember that life is really short. Thirty years out seems like an eternity for a young person but it looks like a mere breath to a person looking back on their lifetime. Most elderly people when they look back at their lives will tell you that life wasn't always easy but that the years went by rapidly. Trust me you will probably get to the place in life when you no longer want to work. The job stress that you easily faced at age thirty five often seems overwhelming in your sixties. If you want to keep working, good for you. My brother-in-law just got a new full time job at age 72 and he is excited and rearing to go. But many don't feel this way about their work when they reach their retirement years. Many retire because they just can no longer handle their work stress. Give yourself the possibility of being able to retire if you want to. Keeping this in mind might help you to be able to discipline yourself to consistently put aside for retirement. Third, remember this that doing the right thing regularly over a long period of times pays great rewards. Eating the right kinds and amounts of food, exercising, and lowering stress over a long period of time results in a trim and healthy body. On the other hand, going to the gym once a year and dieting for one week does nothing for a person. It is the regular and consistent saving for retirement over a long period of time that will help you retire successfully. I never made much money but I practiced this principle and it has allowed me to retire relatively worry free. As a matter of fact, a year into retirement I have not had to touch my retirement savings and my total portfolio has grown. I am not worried about running out of money because I haven't touched my retirement savings yet. I can foresee this pattern happening until I am forced by the government to begin to withdraw at the age of 72 for tax purposes. Anyway, this is a good position to be in. You will be in a similar position if you discipline yourself to save for retirement over many years. If you haven't started saving, do it now. The sooner the better off you will be.

Chapter 11

Apply Wisdom

Anyone can spend money, and it is easy to waste it quickly, as I have stated. But it takes incredible wisdom to learn how to manage one's money and to save and invest for a good retirement. This is especially for true for the little guy who has never made a lot of money but would like to be able to retire comfortably. Again, it is not always a matter of making more money. A lot of people who make three or four times more than what you and I make can't handle their money. They have insurmountable debt, and they are living from paycheck to paycheck. Wisdom is really the key. Knowledge can be acquired (facts, how things work), but wisdom is the ability to use one's knowledge in an effective way. For example, I have a few power tools that I know how to operate (that's knowledge). But I wouldn't have the faintest idea how to use them to build a house, so I wouldn't attempt it (that's wisdom). I'm not a handyman anyway. When I start to fix something my wife calls the prayer chain.

The Bible stresses the importance of wisdom. It says that wisdom is more valuable than silver or gold, and though it costs you all you have, get wisdom (Proverbs 4:7). I used to ask my parishioners if they had the choice between wisdom and a million dollars, which one would they choose. Almost everyone, because we were in church and because they knew what I wanted them to say, claimed that they would choose wisdom. But I doubt that. I believe few people would actually choose wisdom over a million dollars. It is hard for us to believe that wisdom is that valuable. We are so used to believing that nothing in life is as important as the almighty dollar. As I'm writing this, our world is facing the terrible COVID-19 pandemic. People are dying, people are losing their jobs, and people are scared. Recently I heard that we have more people unemployed than there was at the height of the Great Depression.

Money is not the issue. The government has provided stimulus checks and help for small businesses. What we need is wisdom to keep the virus from spreading and causing thousands or even millions from dying. We need wisdom in discovering and creating medications and vaccinations to address the virus. We have the money, but we don't have the wisdom we need to stop this virus. Wisdom truly is more important than money. I bring all of this up because I believe the most important aspect of managing our money is wisdom. Remember, my definition: "Wisdom is the ability to look at life and life's problems from God's point of view." God knows how we should invest and how much we should spend and give. He knows the answer to every problem we have. So we need to get God's wisdom so we will know how to handle our money. There are a lot of people doing stupid things with their money and we don't want to be like them. We need to apply God's wisdom to the handling of our finances. So how do we get God's wisdom? The Bible says that we need to ask him for it.

"Let perseverance finish its work so that you may be mature and complete, not lacking anything. If any of you lacks wisdom, you should ask God, who gives generously to all without finding fault, and it will be given to him. But when you ask, you must believe and not doubt, because the one who doubts is like a wave of the sea, blown and tossed by the wind" (James 1:4–6).

We ask God for wisdom in respect to our finances. The Bible says that if we ask God for it, believing that he will answer us, he will give it to us. There are few days that go by in which I don't ask the Lord to give me wisdom in respect to my finances and other personal matters. It is because of this that I have learned how to live well, within my means and prepare for a good retirement. I'm not just saying this because I am a preacher, and maybe I should quote something from the Bible. The whole reason I have a plan that has worked is because I have wholeheartedly sought God's wisdom each and every day for many years.

There are few days that go by in which I don't ask the Lord to give me wisdom in respect to my finances and other personal matters.

Long ago I heard the following story, which changed my life. Let's just say it became my life story even though it didn't happen to me. But it represented my life, at least the way that I have wanted to live. The man who told the story was about my age, but he was talking about something he heard when he was a teenager. The man said that he was at his friend's house one day and his friend's father was telling about something that happened to him as a soldier during World War II. The friend's father told how he and his company were pinned down behind enemy lines during wintertime. The only way out was to go through an American minefield that was covered with snow. Even though it was an American minefield, no one had the map, so no one knew where the mines were. The troops could either take their chances of going through the minefield or attempt to exit before the enemy, where they would face certain death. The American commander told his men that they were going to walk single file through the minefield. Each man would follow him, 100 feet apart. The commanding officer said, "If I get blown up, follow the man behind me. If he gets blown up, follow the man behind him, and so on." Well, incredibly, the entire company of American soldiers made it safely across that minefield and there wasn't one explosion.

That was the end of the story. The man wasn't making an application or spiritual point. But when I heard it, I thought, "*Oh my, that story is for me. In fact, it is my life's story!*" I told myself that for the rest of my life I would endeavor to follow in the footsteps of my commanding Heavenly Officer. If I stray from his steps there is a good chance I will be exploded by some sinful distraction. In other words, I told myself that I would endeavor to walk in obedience to my Lord's instructions so that I won't have to face the terrible consequences of sin. The Bible says that the wages of sin is death. During my over 40 years of ministry, I have seen people suffer greatly because they have disobeyed God's commandments. The only smart way to live is by walking in his steps.

This is true when it comes to finances. If I handle my money the way God wants me to, I am not going to get blown apart by financial disasters. I won't do something disastrous like buying homes and cars that I can't afford, or investing my retirement funds on a fast horse.

In 2008, I was 12 years from retirement and the economic downturn didn't affect me much. But I remember that there were a lot of people who were just about ready to retire but couldn't because they had lost a third of their retirement investments in the sinking markets. I was determined that would not happen to me. So as I got closer to retirement, I put the far majority of my investments in cash or fixed securities that would be unaffected by a market collapse. Some advisors encouraged me not to be so conservative because they said I would miss out on future market gains. Well, sure enough, the markets have dropped dramatically and it happened in just a few short days. There are a lot of people who were getting ready to retire but who would possibly have to delay because they were too aggressively invested. I'm not saying that I'm a genius or that I'm smarter than everyone else. But I am saying that if we seek God's wisdom, he will guide us and help us to do smarter things with our money.

"Now then, my children, listen to me; blessed are those who keep my ways. Listen to my instruction and be wise; do not disregard it. Blessed are those who listen to me, watching daily at my doors, waiting at my doorway. For those who find me find life and receives favor from the LORD. But those who fail to find me harm themselves; all who hate me love death" (Proverbs 8:32–36).

Chapter 12

Plan the Specifics

To retire or not retire, that is the question. When I was seriously considering retirement I began to research the subject for about five years before I actually took the plunge. I read everything I could on retirement, and I attended seminars and talked to many of the retirees who lived at the retirement center where I worked. Comments were mixed. One person told me, “Oh, you’ll hate it. Retirement was the worst thing I ever did.” Two people in their 90s told me that they didn’t enjoy retirement and would still be working full time if they could. Others told me that they absolutely loved retirement and were convinced that I would too. On one hand, I looked forward to being able to actually retire but, on the other hand, I had a sickening feeling that I would get bored and depressed. I had spoken with three financial advisors (free one-time sessions) and all of them were absolutely convinced that I could make it financially. Still, I was afraid of running out of money, which is one of the greatest fears many retirees face. To make things more complicated, many of my family members and close friends my age were still working and wouldn’t give a thought to retiring. “If you love your work why in the world would you want to retire?” I begin to feel that there was something wrong with me for even considering doing so. I consulted with a few recently retired neighbors. One man said that he was really struggling with boredom and could barely make it through the winter months when he was stuck inside his home. The other neighbor worked until he was 70 and then retired decided to retire. When I asked how he liked retirement he told me, “I love it!” So what was I to do with all this information? Some said they loved it and others hated it.

One of the clinchers in my decision came from another close friend exactly my age. I got to know him because his father is a resident at the retirement village where I worked. The man actually retired a year before I did, and he told me that he had been under great stress emotionally and physically at work. His financial advisor told him that many people are in this situation; this is one of the main reasons people end up retiring as soon as they can. I had to admit that even though I loved what I did, I was feeling a lot of stress because of my job. My body was showing me this as little skin cancers were growing in different places. I was sleeping poorly, getting only 4 or 5 hours of sleep at night. I had to admit, I was under stress. While I admire those who continue to work many years after reaching full retirement age, I was not going to be one of them. My wife's health was a factor in my decision to stay home, and so was the constant reminder that life is short, as I was constantly around death at the retirement center. Life is short for all of us, and at my age I could be very well be missing out on some of the best years of my life. One man at the village told me, "You're doing the right thing in retiring, because the years of 67-72 years of age are the best years of a person's life. They don't have to work and they are still young enough to do things they enjoy." That seemed like really good advice to me because I was certainly aware of the limited activity level of people who were not too much older than this. We also had people in the retirement center my age or younger who had died. I seriously questioned whether I wanted to work the remainder of my best years at a job that was putting me under stress and strain. Perhaps the biggest reason for my decision to retire came from my father's example. My dad retired at the age of 65 from his job as a music professor at a college in downtown Chicago. I was 22 at the time and I remember driving my sister's station wagon to the college and loading my father's office papers and equipment. I could tell he had mixed emotions about retiring. It is scary to go from working everyday to suddenly stopping. Well, things started out good for my parents--as a matter of fact, really good. I had never seen either of my parents so happy. They bought a new car to travel back and forth from Chicago to the trailer they had just purchased in a retirement court in Florida. My father had plans of remodeling a house on his hobby farm. Things were looking good until tragedy struck. While in Florida, my father was bitten by a mosquito carrying something that gave him encephalitis. There were others who died from the same disorder during the same time. My father didn't die, but he was in a state of living that was actually worse than death. For four years he "existed" in a nursing home totally brain damaged until he finally expired at the age of 69. Some retirement! My mother died 3 years later also at the age of 69. Their deaths at relatively young ages by today's standards convinced me that I should give retirement serious consideration

I could tell he had mixed emotions about retiring. It is scary to go from working everyday to suddenly stopping.

To retire or not to retire; that is the question. You may enjoy your job and want to work as long as you can. I know people who have worked well into their 90s. If you want to keep working and you aren't stressed, keep going. Just remember that life is really short and there are no guarantees. If there are things on your bucket list that you really want to do, if you keep working you may never get a chance to accomplish them. I have been retired for a little over a year, and I can absolutely say that it was the right decision for me. My wife needs me home, and I am finding many fun and interesting things to do. Every evening I wonder where the day went. I haven't been bored, and there are plenty of things I am looking forward to doing. Keep in mind that this is during the pandemic, when many businesses and stores, churches, in fact most everything, is shut down. Yet I'm still finding many enjoyable things to do.

I remember being on vacations and getting that sick feeling, *Oh, I've got to go back to work on Monday. I wish I could just stay on vacation.* Now I can. I love getting up in the morning and not having to rush off to work. Recently I was on my bicycle in the middle of the day and I was enjoying the view of the rivers and trees on one of our city's many bike trails. I thought to myself, "I'm so glad that I am retired and I'm so glad I don't have to go back to work." But even if you aren't ready to retire yet, keep this in mind: Someday you may want to. You may wake up one day and think, "Enough is enough, I don't want to work anymore." When this happens you want to be able to, financially and in other ways. It is one thing to work during your retirement age because you want to or because you want a part-time gig to give you something to do. But it is another thing to be 70 years old and want to retire but can't because you need the money. You don't want to be in this position. So I want to conclude this section by identifying some things you will need to do to be able to retire successfully.

A. Figure out Your Finances

You have to figure out if you can afford to retire. As I mentioned before, you figure out your living expenses and weigh them against your fixed income sources--Social Security, pensions, whatever you have. You will have to withdraw the gap amount from retirement savings and/or part-time work. Remember, you can help yourself by lowering your cost of living and by eliminating your debt. There are calculators on the internet that can help you estimate how many years your retirement savings should last.

Amazingly, most of the material I have read and speakers I have heard focus on one aspect of retirement and that is finances. There is much more to it than being financially prepared if we want to have a happy retirement. It is important, and we can't get there without having our financial house in order, but there are some other important things that need to be figured out if we want to be well adjusted in retirement.

B. Plan Your Activities

Years ago I visited a widow who had recently moved into our retirement village, and she began speaking to me about her deceased husband. "You know, Chaplain, when a person retires, they are going to need to have something to do." The emphasis on her sentence was on the "*to do*". I could sense that things had not gone to well in her husband's retirement years and that he became bored and restless, and perhaps that was what contributed to his relatively early death. When the woman made the statement, I got a sick feeling deep inside, because I knew that I was inwardly afraid of having nothing to do in my retirement. I had heard the statistics of how many people, men in particular, struggle emotionally after they retire. I have heard that as many as 40 percent struggle with depression. I had heard stories of how people die shortly after they retire. The widow told me, "Joe worked hard all his life in the factory for 30 years. He retired at 55 because they offered him an early out. But he didn't have any hobbies or interests. All he did was sit around day and night, watching TV. Three years later he died of a stroke." I've heard the stories, and they have frightened me: *Maybe I should just keep working as long as I can.* I admit the fear delayed my retirement for a few months. It is just scary to go from working all your life to suddenly putting the brakes on. Not only do people's activity levels change drastically, but so does their identity. No longer is someone Bob the lawyer or Carol the doctor, or so-and-so the whatever. But now that someone is a retiree, her job is no longer her identity.

"What do you do for a living?" "Oh, I'm retired." "So you must have a lot of time on your hands right?"

The implication is that we're not worth much if we don't have a significant title or position and if we're retired, we're just kind of put out to pasture. There is a lot of rethinking people have to do in terms of their identity and self worth when they enter into retirement. The usual bookstore and internet sources on retirement offer very little to guide a person through this transitioning. There is a plethora of help in terms of financial guidance, but not so much in terms of emotionally adjusting to a completely different way of life and a different way of thinking about who we are. My guess is that the more a person ties his or her self worth to their career, the more difficult the process will be. I also believe that men have a more difficult time than women with this adjustment. Women have a natural mothering and caretaking instinct that men just don't have. Ask anyone who works in a long-term facility; by and large it is the daughters who not only visit but emotionally take on the burden of their elderly parents' care. There are exceptions, but generally the daughters are there sitting with parents for hours on end, running them to doctors' appointments, staying with them overnight when they are in the hospital. In my chaplain ministry I have come to know numerous daughters of our residents. Many of them have fulltime careers, but they naturally take on a caretaking role that a lot of sons just aren't willing to assume. Seeing these women day after day, I would get to know them quite well, but I often wouldn't even meet the sons until the funeral of their elderly parents. There certainly are exceptions. I have also met some wonderful care giving sons, but most people who carry on this role are women. Remember the old saying, "A son is a son until he gets a wife, but a daughter is a daughter for the rest of her life."

An interesting article suggests what many suspect that men on a whole have a more difficult time adjusting to retirement than men. The article suggests several reasons for this one being that women are often better at multitasking responsibilities between work and home and they are often more socially engaged. The article suggests however that given time, men do tend to catch up with women in making a good adjustment to retirement.

(Pascale, Rob Man Vs Woman: Who's Better At Retirement? **Forbes, February 21, 2019, 12;56 p.m.)**

What I did and what I would suggest doing is to make a list (in writing, not just mentally) of the kinds of things you think you might enjoy doing. I wouldn't analyze too much at this point but just brainstorm anything you might think is a possibility. Here is a list, unedited, which I made up several years before I actually retired:

Activities:
House projects:
*Garage: sorting, working on lawn mower, maintaining yard equipment
*Learning new skills: home repair--electrical and plumbing, making toys,
remodeling
*Physical Exercise: Running (hopefully), biking, weights, yoga and stretching,
tennis

Interests: *
*Culture: exploring Des Moines, travel logs to other countries
*Computer: organizing, optimizing, surfing
*History
*Healing
*Prophecy
*Bible
*Genealogy
*Finances, investments
*Visiting older folks--always a passion
*Perhaps a part-time position in a church
*Driving on occasion--pick up a car or deliver a car
*Volunteering--like at Hope Ministries or JCA
*Trees--learning about them, botany
*Take community education classes.

Hobbies:
*Assembling radios
*Assembling electronic boards
*Stereos - fixing
*Assembling toy boats and planes
*Drones
*Assembling computer
*Fishing

I realized at the time I compiled my list that I might not ever do some of it, but I wanted to get the possibilities of the kinds of things I might be interested in down on paper. What I didn't want to do was hit retirement with no idea of what I'd be doing. I also talked to a lot of retirees about the kinds of activities that they enjoyed after they retired. This gave me some good ideas.

Then, as I actually got closer to retirement, I made up another list of activities I was actually more likely to do because they held a greater interest for me. Here is another unedited list:

> **Activities:** bicycling, visitation, learning city--parks museums neighborhoods, taking bus, home maintenance, photography? Radio--Ham and/or assembly? Stereo? Contacting funeral homes for (doing funerals, make up a business card) learn about trees, historical research, genealogy, things to assemble in basement, finding a nursing home where I can do church services and visit, attend sports events cross country and track, girls softball.

When it came time to actually retire, I made another list that included things I was committed to doing. The list included calling elderly friends by phone, staining the decks on the house, getting my yard equipment ready, writing, exercising, house work, changing the oil on the car, organizing my desk and workroom, fine-tuning my budget on my computer, organizing my filing cabinet, bicycling, visiting parks . . .

When I was working, I would have a To-do List for every day of the week. Then I would cross off each activity as I got it done. I decided to not be that regimented during retirement. Instead of having to get certain things on my list done every day and checking everything off, I would have a longer list, and I would mentally think through what I wanted to do each day. This way I would have more flexibility for things that might come up, for example, if Richard called me and wanted to go bicycling. The key for me is knowing what you want to do, being flexible about it, and enjoying it. I feel God saying to me, "Craig, attempt to enjoy rather than to accomplish." When I was working, it was all about accomplishing, and it was all under the pressure of deadlines. Now, I'm trying to forget about deadlines and I am focusing more on enjoying what I am doing. When I was working, I had to get all my personal stuff done in one day, which included errands, household chores, and more. It was all a rush. Now, there are no deadlines and I can enjoy what I am doing. That is a key word for retirement, isn't it? Enjoy.

So how is it working? Amazingly, I am getting a lot accomplished, and I am thoroughly enjoying what I'm doing. Every day I have a list of fun things to do and I haven't been bored yet. At the end of the day, I think to myself, "*Where did the day go?*" I am anticipating that every day will be like this. To me, this makes retirement really fun and exciting, but I want to stress it is our personal responsibility to come up with activities that are enjoyable and fun. No one will do this for us. We are no longer in school or at work where someone told us what to do. We have to take the initiative.

Now there are no deadlines and I can enjoy what I am doing. That is a key word for retirement, isn't it? Enjoy.

I noticed in the nursing home that people who were the happiest and most well adjusted had activities they enjoyed. One lady, 97 years old, a real peach, showed me her puzzles, her word games, and her needlework. She had a computer that she used to email her children and her grandchildren. She would watch the news, and she had favorite TV programs that she watched every day. She read quite a bit. She would always attend Chapel and every activity the center made available. She was happy, because she had a positive attitude and she kept busy. I still love her and miss her and continue to phone her, although I am no longer employed at the retirement center.

Contrast this woman to a man I knew from a former church who just about had a nervous breakdown after he retired. After doing nothing but watch TV in his basement for about six months, he was seriously depressed. His wife called me and asked me to come and visit him, which I did. I had prayer with him and counseled him, but what really helped him was when he began to volunteer at the local hospital, driving people in a little cart from their cars to the facility. He was like a new man, happy and cheerful. The widow was right, "If you're going to retire, you have to have something to do."

C. Determine Where to Live

Recently I spoke on the phone with the daughter of one of our residents. She told me that she and her husband had just retired to Florida and were really enjoying it. Are there better places to live than where you are living? Some states, like Florida and Arizona, cater to retirees in terms of taxes and amenities. It is exciting to think of retiring to some warmer climate, and a lot of people do it and are really happy. Some do it, however, and are not so happy. After they move they discover that they miss their families and the friendships they have had for many years. This is something to think through carefully. It would be wise to visit somewhere for a few weeks to see if you really like it. A lot of the retirees I have spoken to enjoyed snow-birding in places like Florida, south Texas, and Arizona. It sounds like a fun way to go. You can keep your friendships and family connections back home and get out of the northern winters. I'm still thinking of this possibility for myself.

What you live *in* is also an important consideration for a retiree. It may be time to get rid of the large home and get a cheaper and more manageable place to live. You may want to contemplate living in a condo or a ranch home. Wherever you go, make sure it is a place that has no or very few stairs. You may be able to negotiate them today but, in a year or two, you might find them more difficult, even dangerous. Someone suggested that when you purchase a home, you want to think about what kind of health you may face in 5 or 6 years. This kind of eliminates purchasing that beautiful acreage that requires lot of yard work. At age 65 a person might be able to maintain it, but probably not at 70 and older.

Retirement centers like the one I worked in are a viable option for some retirees. One lady told me that she would go for days without ever talking with a human being when she lived in her townhome. But this all changed when she moved into the retirement center. There she made all kinds of friends, and there were plenty of activities to keep her busy when she wanted to do things. A lot of people like the continuum of care that a long-term facility offers. They start in independent living and can move on to assisted living and then the nursing home, if need be. It is important for a lot of people not to have to leave one retirement facility to go to another one. Keep in mind that the older we get, the less change appeals to us, and the harder it is to move.
Retirement centers are not for everyone, however. Some people move into them and quickly move out. Many miss their homes and their previous activities. One man told me he was leaving the

independent unit because he missed his garage and his tools. The three most common complaints that I heard from our residents were: the escalating rent increases, poor maintenance when things broke down, and too many rules. Retirement centers are expensive. Someone has to pay for all those employee salaries (we had 190 employees in ours), and that is going to be the renters. A lot of people feel too restricted by the rules of the facility. One lady told me after she moved into assisted living, "It's fine, but I like to be the boss." It is true, the higher you go in the level of care you will need, the less freedom and more rules you will have. One man jokingly said he was not living in assisted living, but rather "restricted living."

Retirement centers are expensive. Someone has to pay for all those employee salaries . . . and that is going to be the renters.

I would check around if you are interested in a retirement center. They can vary a lot. Some offer many more activities and have more amenities. For example, some have chapel services, swimming pools, exercise rooms, wood shops, libraries, even golf courses. These are often more expensive. Here is an editorial thought that many people will take offense to: My belief is, since most of the activities departments in retirement centers are staffed by women, they naturally design activities that appeal to women. They may occasionally have an outing to see a ballgame, but largely they present activities that don't interest men. I've seen it many times: women gathered around a table with the activities director, who is showing them how to make doilies or Christmas ornaments. Where I worked, I suggested that maybe they could have a craft like assembling model cars or airplanes. My suggestion didn't go over too well. I proposed that we have a shop where men could make wood projects. I was told insurance would be a problem. It didn't seem to be a problem in some other retirement centers. I would definitely keep this in mind if I were checking out a retirement facility: Are the activities offered to men as well as to women? Having something to do is very important, and I saw more than a few bored men in the retirement center where I worked.

I would definitely keep this in mind if I were checking out a retirement facility: Are the activities offered to men as well as to women?

Some centers have you pay an endowment, like maybe $200,000, before you move in. On top of this you will pay your rent, which is also very high. That just doesn't seem like a good deal for me or the other little guys like me. I have a friend however, whose father lives in such a facility, and he loves it.

Many people prefer to stay in their home, and I am one of them. An older gentleman that I know suggests says that a person can stay in their home and hire housekeepers and yard workers for a lot less money than it costs to live in a retirement center. There is truth to what he says. One woman from our center complained about missing her home the whole five years she was a resident. She told me before she died, "Pastor, stay in your home for as long as you can." Another woman came into our facility kicking and screaming. Her children arranged the move, and she was mad at all of them. She had lived in her home for 92 years. She was born in her home. All she ever wanted to talk about was moving back to it.

In our city, there are apartments and cottages exclusively for people 55 and over. They offer the benefit of supplying a social network, but without the overhead costs. Some of them are income based. I would consider moving into one of these facilities before I would move into a retirement center. I have friends who have moved into one, and they remark about how friendly everyone is and how they are developing a great sense of community.

The last thing I would say about housing is this: Where you choose to live is very important. One lady told me that she lived in senior housing and it was filled with people doing drugs. She feared for her life. Never move to a place where you don't feel safe. In spite of its affordability or activity level, if it is unsafe, forget it. We may have been able to handle things like that when we were younger, but in our old age we are a lot more vulnerable.

This book is about how I have made good financial moves that have set me up well for retirement. I have not always done everything right, however. One of the biggest mistakes I have ever made has been in the area of housing. I'm talking about where I am living right now. Economically, it was a great deal. I live in a brand new house, all on one floor, two bathrooms, washer and dryer on the main floor. We have brand new appliances; in fact, brand new everything. Because the house is located in a developing city neighborhood, we have a ten year tax abatement, which is huge especially for retirees. The city also gave us $10,000 to use for upgrades on the house in any way we want. We don't have to pay the money back if we stay here five years. They gave us $2,500 for closing costs. The house came fully landscaped and with a fully sodded lawn. I bought the home for less than the asking price and was able to have them throw in extras like ceiling fans and appliances. It was the deal of deals, but there was one problem: The location. Not only are we living in a higher crime area of the city, but it is terribly noisy. I began to notice how noisy it was from the nearby traffic when I came by to survey the building progress. *"It is really noisy here",* I thought. *"I'm not sure if I can live with this."* Even though I had not given the builders any money at that point, I had given them my word. They had already made some modifications I requested in the home. Legally I could have gotten out of the deal, but I didn't feel I could ethically. So, here we are in this beautiful house, the perfect retiree home, but I deal daily with motorcycles, trucks, cars without mufflers, noises practically right in my living room. My wife rarely notices it, and friends that visit say it doesn't bother them. Neighbors say the noise doesn't affect them, but it does me. It has been a struggle, and I'm presently trying to sell the home by owner, but there hasn't been much interest. What my mother said to me when I was looking to purchase my first house is really true: "Location, location, location." Choose where you decide to live very carefully. You might not be able to get out of it very easily. I've heard of people from northern states moving down to sunshine states after they retired. Some loved it and never looked back but others returned up north after a year or two of hating where they lived. Think of the trouble and expense these folks went through. It would be hard even on young people but much more so on retirees. You want to avoid mistakes like this. Think through where you want to live carefully.

D. Focus on Spiritual Riches

Some people don't seem to have a spiritual bone in their body. They never think about God or where they are going to spend eternity. One day, a preacher that visited an older man from his community. This man did not attend a church and did not seem to have an interest in spiritual matters. So the pastor asked the elderly gentleman, "Mr. Smith, do you ever think about the hereafter?" "As a matter of fact I do, Rev," replied the man. "I get up from watching the TV and go into the living room to get something, and I start wondering what I'm here after. This happens to me almost every day. So yes, I think about the hereafter quite a bit." Some people just don't get it, do they?

Jesus spoke about a man who was very much like Mr. Smith in terms of spiritual matters:

> And he told them this parable: "The ground of a certain rich man yielded an abundant harvest. He thought to himself, 'What shall I do? I have no place to store my crops.'
>
> "Then he said, 'This is what I'll do. I will tear down my barns and build bigger ones, and there I will store my surplus grain. And I'll say to myself, "You have plenty of grain laid up for many years. Take life easy; eat, drink and be merry."'
>
> "But God said to him, 'You fool! This very night your life will be demanded from you. Then who will get what you have prepared for yourself?'
>
> "This is how it will be with whoever stores up things for themselves but is not rich toward God." (Luke 12:16–21)

In his story about the "rich fool," Jesus stressed the importance of tending to spiritual matters. The painful reality is, we are all going to die and we are going to have to be accountable before God for the way we have lived our lives. To write a book on retirement and not even give mention to the most important thing we need to prepare for is preposterous.

Years ago, I had lunch with a successful young banker who had just started attending the church where I was a pastor. The man told me how he had everything figured out in terms of his future, which included his savings plan, his retirement, and his legal will--everything. He had his future entirely mapped out, but he had forgotten the most important detail: Where he was going to spend eternity.

A TV commercial years ago, featured a man verbally giving his grocery list to a grocer in a small store where the man had shopped for years. The grocer, astonished, asked him, "How did you do it? How did you give me the whole list by memory? You usually have to write everything down, and even then you have to come back to the store because you've forgotten something. So how did you do it?" The man said, "Easy, I took a 35-day memory course." "Very impressive," said the grocer. But as the customer, holding his grocery sack, turned around to leave the store, the camera showed that he had forgotten the most important thing--his pants.

More important than having a good financial plan and a good retirement strategy, in fact the most important thing is knowing where we are going to spend eternity.

As I have previously stated, I regret not having been able to travel more. Part of my problem is that I am terrible at packing a suitcase and figuring out what I will need when I finally get to my destination. I always seem to forget the most important things. It started way back when I was a child, about seven years old. My father, being cheap like me, didn't take us on expensive vacations. Our yearly vacation was to go from Chicago, where we lived, to Des Moines to visit my grandparents. My dad was 43 years older than me, so my grandparents and all the relatives seemed really old from my young perspective. I loved them all, but there just wasn't much that a kid my age could do for fun. I had two sisters, but they were older and kind of in a different world. So I was just plain bored. On one particular trip to Des Moines, at seven years of age, I told my mother I would pack my own suitcase. Either she didn't hear me or she was too busy to notice. But I packed my suitcase totally full of toys. The only clothes I had were the ones on my back. I was determined not to be bored stiff at granddad's house, like I was the year before. I can still hear my mother screaming on Sunday morning when she opened up my suitcase to get my clothes ready for church. There was a lot of scrambling around, and of course no one wore my size. So my father had to make a run to the store to get me something to wear.

I'm a little better in preparing for trips today, but not much, to be honest with you. I will always forget something; you can ask my wife. It might be my toothbrush or my shoes or a shirt, but it is just about a sure bet that I will forget something. I try to compensate by bringing extra pants and shirts, everything I can think of, but I will invariably forget something important. The worst came just a few years ago when a very good friend from a former church asked me to come and conduct the funeral of his wife, who had tragically passed away. The morning of the funeral I discovered that I had forgotten my suit and my dress shoes. My friend had an extra suit, but it was way too small for me. So, what could I do but conduct the funeral in my blue jeans, t-shirt, and tennis shoes? I explained to the church that I wasn't trying to be disrespectful, but that I had simply forgotten my suit. I had laid it out with my dress shoes but somehow, I had forgotten to put them in the car. The people understood and thought it was pretty funny. I had been their pastor for 18 years, so they were kind of used to the dumb things I could do.

I tell you this story to let you know that I am not good at packing or planning trips. I would starve as a travel agent. But I do know how to tell people how to prepare for the most important trip of all, that is, how to prepare for eternity.

I am not good at packing or planning trips. . . . But I do know how to tell people how to prepare for the most important trip of all . . . how to prepare for eternity.

Each of us needs to get right with God. We need to receive his son, Jesus Christ, as our personal savior, and we need to live our lives for him. I know that we live in a day and age where "tolerance" is king. The idea is that every religious view is true if the person truly believes in their religious perspective. Who are we to say that our way is true and all the other religions are wrong? This is the thinking of our day that all religions are true and all paths lead to the same destination. It is seen as offensive to challenge someone else's religious view. So would you challenge someone who sincerely thought that they could take any road going south in Iowa and somehow make it to Canada? No matter how sincere someone is in their belief, all roads do not lead to the same destination. Jesus said that he is the only way to salvation and eternal life: "Jesus answered, 'I am the way and the truth and the life. No one comes to the Father except through me'" (John 14:6).

It is okay to make some financial mistakes along the way. It is okay to make some slip-ups retirement planning. It is not okay to make a mistake about where a person will spend eternity. Who cares if someone gains the whole world if they lose their soul? (See Mark 8;36.) Don't be a fool. Make sure you know you are going to spend eternity in heaven.

Recently on the news, it was reported that a well-known comedian had died of natural causes. The man was in his nineties. His wife, also a comedian, had preceded him in death a few years before. The newscaster closed his report by stating, "I bet the man and his wife are going to be laughing together for eternity." Maybe, or maybe not. It depends on where they are. Not everyone goes to heaven; some, according to the Bible, will suffer in hell. We don't want to go there and we don't have to. If we want to spend eternity in heaven, we can do something about it.

Here's a prayer I've said in church many times. It is specifically for people who don't know where they're going to spend eternity and want to get right with God:

> Lord Jesus, I believe that you are the Son of God. I thank you for dying on the cross for my sins. I ask you on the basis of what you have done for me to forgive me for my sins and to save me from going to hell. I receive you into my life, and I put my trust in you as opposed to my own works. Jesus, I give my life entirely to you. In your name, Amen.

If this prayer speaks to you, say it and believe it, and Jesus will receive you into his kingdom when you die. I have led perhaps hundreds of people in a prayer similar to this during my ministry. Some have made noticeable changes in their lives as they have fully placed their trust in Jesus for their salvation. Others, after saying the prayer, have continued on just as they were before. The mystery of this was brought out to me years ago when I led a weekly Bible study at a county jail in southern Iowa. The far majority of the inmates that I encouraged to say a similar prayer told me that they had already done it. Many of them knew the most famous Bible verse on the subject of salvation: "For God so loved the world that he gave his one and only Son, that whoever believes in him should not perish but have eternal life" (John 3:16).

Something was not right here. Sometime in their lifetimes before being sent to jail, they had understood that salvation was not a matter of good deeds but rather trusting in Christ's good works. They had asked Jesus to forgive them, and they had prayed to receive him by faith, but they were leading lives of crime.

All this is to say that receiving salvation involves more than rattling off a prayer. It involves sincerity of heart, and it involves repentance. Jesus said that we would know a tree by its fruit. In other words, people who are ready for their final destination live like they are ready. They do good works and act out of selflessness as opposed to living lives of hatred, selfishness, and crime.

Even doing good works doesn't ensure that someone is truly saved and bound for heaven. Years ago, a notorious crime boss gave thousands of dollars of free food away. His benevolence didn't change who he really was. It was kind of like putting perfume on a skunk.

The true test of whether someone belongs to God and is destined to be with him after they die is this: God's people have his Spirit living in them. Whoever has the Son has life; whoever does not have the Son of God does not have life" (1 John 5:12). That is the test. If you have the Son, or God's Spirit, living inside of you, you have eternal life. If you don't, you don't have eternal life. The next verse tells us that when we have Jesus living inside of us, we will know for sure that our eternal destination with God is sealed: "I write these things to you who believe in the name of the Son of God so that you may *know* that you have eternal life." (1 John 5:13, emphasis mine). This is important, because so many retirees have told me that they hope they are going to heaven when they die. The Bible says, however, that we can know. We know because we have Christ's Spirit living inside of us. His Spirit bears witness with our spirit that we belong to him: "The Spirit himself testifies with our spirit that we are God's children" (Romans 8:16). This means God's children have an inner awareness that they belong to him. The awareness is given to them through the Holy Spirit. How do we receive his Spirit? We turn to Christ and turn away from sin. We put our trust in him for our salvation, and we give our lives fully to him.

I first became aware of Christ living in me when I was 15 years of age. Many times I had said a similar prayer to the above mentioned one. But I was not sincere and had no intention of living according to God's expectations. When I finally fully surrendered my life to him, I began to notice that there was someone living inside of me. I had never before heard anyone suggest this could happen to a person, even though I had been raised in the church. Christ living inside of me came as a pleasant surprise and has made all the difference in my life. We will know that we are destined for heaven when we have him living inside of us. There are some things that make Christianity unique. All other religions teach that we get to the next level beyond this life by good works. The Bible, however, teaches that we get to heaven by trusting in Christ's good works. Islam, for example, teaches the weighing of the scales. If your good works outweigh your bad, you are bound for Paradise. Reincarnation is very similar. If you do good things you will come back in a higher form in the next life. If you do bad things, you will return to this earth as a bug or a worm. I heard a man who believed in reincarnation being interviewed on the radio. The interviewer asked, "Do you mean to tell me if I eat hamburgers, I'm going to be reincarnated as a worm?" The man replied, "Well it depends how many you eat!" All religions except Christianity hold to this basic premise that our good deeds get us to the next level.

The second way that Christianity is unique is that it teaches, as I have mentioned, that Christ lives within us. Pantheism is the belief that God is everything, the rocks, the clouds, people, animals etc. But that is different from Christianity, which is the only religion that teaches that God comes to live inside us when we receive his Son. Daoism teaches that people can have the Dao inside of them, but very few if any of its followers have claimed to have received it.

I say all of this to remind us once again that it is foolish to be "sitting pretty" in retirement if we are not prepared to meet God in the next life. There are some very good reasons to believe the principles of Christianity and that Jesus is truly the only way to eternal life. I trust you will not allow the thinking of this world to deceive you from these most important truths. Eternity is a long time, and we want to make sure that we will be spending it in the right place.

I want to end this section with something I saw on the Internet several years ago. A man was telling how he went from being an atheist to a union-card carrying Christian. He was a professor at Berkley University and derived great pleasure in belittling Christian students in his classroom. But he found himself on the operating table going in and out of life because of a sudden heart attack. As the medical personnel furiously tried to save his life, the atheist saw himself entering into hell. He didn't believe in God, and he didn't believe in hell, but he saw himself there. He said that it was the most terrifying, horrific place one could ever imagine. He cried out to the Jesus he had not believed in, and he came back to life. The first thing he did as he recovered was to receive Jesus as his Savior and Lord. He became a new man. Not only had this former atheist become a believer, he began to tell everyone who would listen to him about his experience. He said he became a witnessing fanatic and would walk up to perfect strangers and warn them about the horrors of hell. For about a year, the man said that he was totally obnoxious. But it was because of what he had seen and experienced while on that operating table. All potential retirees need to be prepared not just for their golden years but for eternity.

Jesus said that some believe because of what they have seen, but blessed are those who believe even though they haven't seen. I trust that even those who have not had visions or out-of-body experiences will still believe the realities of God's Word and be prepared for the next life.

Our spiritual lives are most important as we age, but other aspects of life are also imperative to living well.

E. Develop a Social Network

For a lot of people, their social life consists of the people they work with. But after they retire, these relationships kind of fade away. So we have to work hard to develop friendships. It is not good to be old and alone. We all need people to interact with. My observation is that women are more naturally adept at doing this. My wife, for example, speaks to her close friends almost every day on the phone. Women come over for coffee, and they love to go places together. Everywhere I have lived I have observed this. Women are communal by their very nature; they love to congregate and to care for one another's needs. For years I conducted a Bible study at a county jail for men and women. In the women's group I was taken aback by how they cared for and nurtured each other. During one session, one of the younger women put her head on the shoulder of one of the older inmates who began to tenderly comfort her. They may have been criminals, but they still retained their nurturing instincts. I have observed the same thing among elderly retirees. Women in their eighties and nineties regularly taking walks together, meeting in each other's apartments just to chat. I have a theory that this could be a reason women tend to live longer and seem as a whole to adjust to retirement better than men. They are by their very nature companionable. Men tend to be loners. We don't make social connections as readily. When we do engage, we usually do so over activities. It is more difficult for us to share our feelings. Men who say they have friends often refer to an old friend they knew many years before from the service or from college days. Even though they haven't talked to each other for years, they still consider the person their best friend. Most women would never go for this. They require more social engagement, and they need to have someone with whom they can share the deep feelings of their hearts. There are exceptions to what I am saying about men and women, but generally it holds true.

Therefore, men in particular have to really be intentional about making social connections during their retirement years. The relationships at work are gone, so how do we go about connecting interactively with others? Well there are a lot of ways. We could visit the senior centers that many communities have. We could do some volunteer work. We could get involved in the church. I, for one, made a list of seniors that I want to visit in their homes. But as soon as I retired, we were hit with the pandemic, so visiting was out of the question. Consequently, I have started phoning people. I also have a friend, Richard, with whom I bicycle on a weekly basis. I have called some people that I've known through my work and have asked them to be part of a weekly small group, where we can share with each other what is going on in our lives. I also keep in close contact with some of my male friends from years past. With modern technology, programs like Zoom, we are now able to keep in contact with people from almost anywhere. The point is, we have to be intentional. We have to make a plan to develop a social network during our retirement years. No one will do it for us. It is our responsibility. I am convinced it is a necessary part of having a healthy and happy retirement. Many retirees move to ideal retirement spots for warmer weather and a lower cost of living. Some end up returning because they missed friends and family. It is something that needs to be thought through; because having a social network is something we are all going to need in retirement.

When my wife and I were first married, a young man befriended us. He asked us to go to concerts and out to dinner with him. It was just the three of us. Although he had only lived in the area for several months, he seemed to have more friends than me, even though I had lived there my entire life. I asked him one day,

"Daryl, how come you have so many friends?" He told me, "Well, they're not going to come to you." That was all he said and all he needed to say. It is up to us if we are going to have friends in our retirement years or if we are going to go it alone.

F. Maintain Good Health

Health is more important than finances when you think about it. Which would you rather be: a wealthy person who is confined to his or her bed, or a healthy person who subsists on a low but sustainable income? I would choose good health any day, and I imagine you would too. I have known some relatively well-to-do people about my age or younger, but they were confined to wheel chairs or hospital beds. This is not the lifestyle you and I would prefer in retirement. Because of this, we need to do all we can to sustain good health. We will enjoy our retirement a lot more if we are healthy. If you are overweight (and a lot of us Americans are), please take steps to get your weight under control through eating changes, or exercise, medication or counseling. A lot of health problems like diabetes, heart disease, and strokes are caused by obesity. In our culture, one of the hardest things is to eat right. There are just too many temptations around us. I have known people, even young people, who have died because of being overweight.

A young, successful businessman from a community where I formerly lived was enormously overweight. I would see him often at the YMCA. He was working out on a somewhat regular basis, but he just couldn't get his eating under control. I asked him one day if he did any sports when he was in high school or college. His answer amazed me. He told me that he used to run cross country. I was an avid runner in high school and college and, let me tell you, I never once saw a fat cross-country runner. When it comes to weight, it doesn't matter what you did in the past however. Everything is based upon what you are doing today. Well, this former cross-country runner, even though he was still in his 30s, just dropped dead from a heart attack one day. I met another man at the gym who was very overweight. He was almost too heavy to straddle the bench in the locker room. He told me that he "used to" run marathons. The lesson is that we have to choose to eat right now, every day. I have noticed that this is harder for me now since I have been retired. When I was working, I was so busy I usually didn't have time to eat lunch. But now, since I am home, I am around food all day long. It is just too easy to munch on cookies and other high-calorie foods. As a person who has exercised regularly all of my life and still continue to, I can attest to the truth that the very "best exercise is pushing yourself away from the table." The over-eating monster needs to be conquered. Support groups like Over-eaters Anonymous" can be very helpful to some people. However, studies have shown that diets don't work very well for most people in the long run. Most people, even if they have gotten down to their desired weight through dieting, will quickly gain it back and more. I've done this haven't you? The best thing is to make eating right part of your lifestyle. Yes, I realize that overeating is not the only reason for being overweight. One's genetic makeup, their medication, or their personal metabolism can all be factors in one's weight. I'm not trying to condemn anyone. But the point is that diets don't often work in the long run. So we need to come up with a plan that is reasonable, one that we can live with. If it is too drastic, like just eating only salad, we're not going to be able to stick with it.

Years ago, I watched a TV program on the morbidly obese. The morbidly obese are people who are 500 to 1,200 pounds. Some of them just stayed in bed all day. They were too heavy to do anything else. They couldn't even get out of the door of their homes. I remember one lady was so heavy workers had to remove her window from the home and take her out with a crane. Another man was 1,200 pounds and nearly dead from his tremendous obesity. He joined a program and began to exercise and diet. He got down to 185 pounds. He was actually the "poster boy" for a national fitness program. But when he met his weight goal, he went out and celebrated. He ordered a huge ice cream sundae. That one little indulgence reopened the floodgates to his poor eating habits. He was soon back up to 1,200 pounds and staying at a treatment center for people with morbid obesity. The director at the center said, "I hope we can save his life." Isn't that totally depressing? The lesson is to not go on a diet but make eating right part of your lifestyle.

Exercise is important also, and I am continuing to do it as long as I possibly can. I ran my last 5K about three years ago. Running was my sport, and I did it as much as 14 miles a day at one point in my life. But over the years, running has taken its toll and has caused some injuries. If you run, I would encourage doing it in moderation, because the pounding will have an effect if you do it too much. I would recommend some low-impact activities, like bicycling, which I do 3 or 4 times a week. Swimming is a great exercise because it is low impact and it benefits many parts of the body. I used to swim a mile a day, that is 36 laps in an Olympic sized pool. I met people who were in their nineties who swam almost every day. One elderly gentleman at the pool said, "You use it or you'll lose it." That's about the short and sweet of it. Do something, walk, go to the gym, play pickle ball. Don't just sit in your chair, because you will lose body function. There are great incentives for seniors to exercise. Some gyms offer discounts or even free memberships to seniors. My city has senior centers that offer exercise classes. You can also find all kinds of exercise classes on the internet. It is up to you and me as to whether we are going to exercise or just sit around.

G. Navigate Medicare

As we all know, the costs of healthcare are escalating in our nation.

We sign up for Medicare Part A when we turn 65. If we wait too long, there are some hoops that have to be gone through to get in. Then it is up to us whenever we want to sign up for Part B.

Medicare Part A covers hospital expenses, hospice, and home healthcare. Medicare Part B, on the other hand, covers outpatient medical care such as doctor visits, x-rays, blood-work, and routine preventative care. The two programs function as two halves of a comprehensive healthcare solution.

Then, once we get Medicare A and B, we will need to get a supplemental plan to cover what Medicare does not. There are two kinds of insurance plans that will supplement this: Medicare Advantage or Medigap (Supplemental) plans. Medicare Advantage plans cost less but are more limited in coverage. They also limit your selection of doctors. Medigap plans cost more, but they cover more. The insurance companies that offer these plans offer the same coverage, but they don't cost the same. Some offer a lower premium initially, but they can increase in cost tremendously over the years. There are different types of plans that we can pay for within our supplemental coverage. For example, Plan F covers a lot and has no deductible while Plan G covers the same but has a deductible. None of the supplemental plans cover medication costs. So we have to get Medicare Plan D (drugs) which is a separate additional monthly cost. A lot of people have their supplemental plan with one insurance company and their drug plan with another company. The reason is because it may be cheaper to do so. My wife and I are on the same Medigap program, but we use different insurance companies for our drug coverage, because I hardly have any medications, one pill to be exact. Mary has many pills she takes morning and night. Her company was better for a person who uses many medications, while mine was cheaper for someone like me.

A lot of people have their supplemental plan with one insurance company and their drug plan with another company.

It is confusing; I'm the first to admit it. The government can't do anything simply. But there are a couple of things we can do to make it understandable. First, states offer free programs that explain Medicare options. I sat down with a volunteer from SHIIP (State of Iowa Insurance Division), who explained my options. It helped a lot. Then you can speak to insurance representatives who sell the supplemental plans. I went with an online broker who took all our information and pointed me to the best company that would meet our needs. This particular broker will answer questions during the year for free as well. For example: "I just got this medical bill, and I'm not sure if I need to pay it or will insurance be paying it?" They will check it out and tell you what you need to do. Last year, Mary and I were on vacation, and she lost her insulin. So I went to the drugstore to pick up two bottles. I was speechless when the pharmacist said, "That will be $675." I didn't even say anything. I just walked out of the store, leaving the man holding the bag. When I got back to the motel, I called our online Medicare broker, who told me she would look into it and call me back. Five minutes later, she gave me the address of another drug-store which I went to and received 2 bottles of insulin for under $100. I would advise checking into an online Medicare broker, because they represent so many different companies and can find you the best deal. I would also recommend one that will have your back in case any problems should arise. However, I have had a difficult time getting hold of someone to talk to from the company during the fall when people usually review their plans.

The last thing I would say about Medicare is to try before you buy. What I mean is, the year before you retire, stop your work insurance and go on Medicare. That will help you know exactly what your medical costs and coverage will be when you finally do retire. You won't have to begin retirement having no idea what Medicare will cover for you. When you do retire, you will be able to set up your budget already knowing what your medical costs will probably be. This is what I did, and it really helped me with my budgeting. Medicare does not cover dental and vision, (some Medicare Advantage plans do) but I was able to keep this coverage while I was working and had the option of paying separately for it when I retired.

H. Consider Those Who Come After You

1. Insurance

Insurance is a necessity. If we own cars and property, we need to have them insured. I knew a man who lost in a fire his entire 18-wheel truck and cab that he owned free and clear because he didn't have insurance. He told me that he was just about to get insurance but hadn't quite gotten around to it. Another man bought a brand new car and paid cash, but didn't have it insured. He was in an accident and had to pay the body shop out of pocket to fix his vehicle. I told him, "You know, if you have a new car, you really have to have insurance." I don't think I convinced him, however.

We all need insurance, but there is such a thing as being insurance poor. This means our insurance premiums are so high that we can't pay for other necessities or we can't afford to put money in our savings accounts. We all need insurance, but we have to be careful that our premiums don't break the bank.

All retirees need to consider life insurance. While we were working and raising a family, we needed it to take care of our loved ones in case we passed away. We also needed disability insurance in case we weren't able to work and provide for our families. When we are retired, do we need coverage? We certainly don't need disability insurance, because our retirement income is not based on our ability to work. Life insurance is the big question. I have a retired friend who has millions of dollars of coverage so his wife will be in better shape when he passes. That is fine, if a person can afford the premiums. Most life insurance premiums get more expensive as we age. One line of reasoning is that we won't need life insurance if our spouses can survive on our retirement earnings. Keep in mind, however, that the amount they get from Social Security will be less when we die. She will get hers or yours, whichever one is greater, but she won't get both. A life insurance policy might be a good idea, depending on your situation. I took out a $250,000 policy on myself, which will last about 10 years. It costs me about a thousand a year. It would help my wife a lot if I die. If Mary died before me, I would not continue my policy. My children are working, and I don't need to have a policy for them. But this is me; you might see it differently. There are also different types of life insurance policies, term and whole life. Some can be cashed in if the policyholder becomes terminal or disabled. They are worth looking into as long as they fit into the retiree's budget and overall needs.

2. Wills and Legal Matters

When I first started working at the retirement village, I was surrounded by people dying, as one would expect working with the elderly. I thought it might be a good idea to get my house in order regarding what my desires are for when I pass. Throughout the years I have known some who have died and have left their spouse in a mess because they didn't have their house in order. We retirees should have a will to designate where we want our money, property, and personal effects to go. It is a good idea to have a "living will," which designates what we want medical personnel to do with us should we become seriously sick (Do or Do Not Resuscitate). They might be able to save our lives after an accident, but do we want to live the rest of our lives as a vegetable? A Power of Attorney gives the authority to a particular person to make legal decisions should we come incapacitated. I found a local lawyer who specializes in preparing these materials, and he did it all for me for $600. He said he didn't make any money on the service but hoped that his clients would return to him for other legal matters. I spoke with an attorney who taught the preparing of wills and similar legal documents to law students at the local university. He told me that a person should review their will yearly. The reason is because, if people that we will money have died when our will is being executed, the entire process gets delayed.

Say you leave some money to Cousin Benny, but Cousin Benny dies. Where does that money you willed to him go? It gets complicated so, according to this attorney who taught this kind of stuff at the local law school, it is best to review one's will yearly. I would encourage you not to try to set this up on your own. There are downloadable legal programs that assist you in making your own will. I wouldn't want to trust something this important to a do-it-yourself will, which may or may not be legal. It is better to pay and make sure we're getting the real deal. Go to a reputable lawyer, one who specializes in wills and estates. He or she can also help with minimizing the taxes that will be incurred after death. It is our responsibility to take care of all these legal matters. I have met people in their eighties who have never given a thought to having a will. We just have to take care of it, the sooner the better. We never know when our time will come.

3. Record Keeping

On occasion my mother would make me sit down go through her legal papers. "Now here is where my bank books are, and here is the copy of the will. Here's the key to the lock box." (By the way, get the name of your kid or someone whom you trust on your lock box. It is a legal nightmare to get it opened if only the names of dead people are on the safety deposit box.) I didn't like it when Mother had these discussions with me, because I didn't want to think about my parents dying. But I'm glad she was so organized and took the time to explain everything. After they passed, their good record keeping, along with a great lawyer, made the disbursement of their estate go very smoothly. I was the executor of the estate, and I don't know what I would have done if she hadn't had everything spelled out so clearly.

I have taken my mother's example but I actually I have done it more thoroughly. I have listed all my accounts on paper, where the will is and all the legal matters for my boys, and I have gone over it with them. I have included what bills need to be paid on a monthly basis and what account they come out of. I have given the name of the attorney and the passwords to my computer programs. Furthermore, I have updated this important information whenever I have made changes. For example, when I retired, I moved my 401(k) from my employer to another company. I included this information on the instructions. The information also includes doctors' names and phone numbers and how to access our living will in case we become incapacitated. It is all on paper, and it will make it all doable for our children when we pass. We don't want to leave them with another burden on top of the grief that they will be carrying.

I favor staying in my home as long as possible. But one of the advantages of living in a retirement center is that our kids don't have property to sell once we pass. If you do decide to stay in your home, you might want to eliminate clutter so your kids won't have to go through so much when you're gone. As I mentioned, my parents had tons of stuff that they left when they passed. Fortunately, for me, I had just moved out of the area and my brother-in-law got stuck getting rid of everything! I still kind of chuckle when I think about it, but I know it was not so funny for him. It is no laughing matter for our adult children if they have to wade through mountains of odds and ends and try to fix up an old house to get ready to sell. We want to make it easier for our loved ones when we pass. Some people move into retirement centers largely to take a burden off their children. One woman told me after she had moved her parents to an assisted living facility, "Now I don't have to worry about them 24 hours a day." As we get older, where we live, what we have, our record keeping doesn't affect just us. It concerns our kids. This is something to think about, not just what's best for us but what's best for our loved ones.

Chapter 13

Look at Retirement from Eternity

Our society tends to value people on the basis of their material wealth. We use the expression, "How much is so and so worth?" If he or she is worth 15 or 20 million, we are really impressed. Jesus said, however, that a person's worth is not based on an abundance of possessions (Luke 12:15). I agree totally. Someone can have very little and be rich in other ways, in terms of their service for others, or in terms of their love and devotion to God. To me, these things are a lot more important than having a lot of money and a "good retirement."

A. Real Heroes

I heard a man on the radio talking about his upcoming lunch appointment with a billionaire. The man was like a kid on Christmas morning. He could hardly wait to meet with this man and pump him with all kinds of questions. "How did you do it? What advice do you have for me?"

Frankly, rich people don't impress me, and neither do people who have been successful in their fields: sports, the arts, ministry, or whatever. In my estimation true heroes are those who have faced all kinds of tragedy but are extremely well adjusted and happy. I spoke of three financial heroes earlier, but I hold these people in even higher esteem. My sister and her husband have been through all kinds of adversity, in fact a lot of it happened in just a few years. They lost their 40-year-old son to a rare form of leukemia. He left behind three little children. They faced financial disaster. My sister had a bout with cancer. They faced other family problems that would have broken many people. Yet my sister and her husband are two of the happiest people you could ever meet. They have a strong faith in Jesus Christ, and they have a great attitude. Yet not all Christian people are happy. Richard Wurmbrand, in his book "*Tortured for Christ,*" tells how he spent many years as a prisoner in a Russian Gulag. When he got out and met with other Christians from the community, he wrote that he was shocked by their lack of joy. Now that causes a person to take pause. Here is a man who is tortured for his faith, but he has joy. When he gets out of prison, he can't understand why other believers don't also have joy. These are my heroes, people who have joy in adversity. (Wurmbrand, Richard, Tortured for Christ, Living Sacrifice Book Company, Barelesville, OK 1967)

One of the workers at the retirement center was trying to think of the name of one of our residents but couldn't come up with it. She described the lady to me, but I wasn't coming up with it either. Finally she said, "You know that person who complains all the time." I finally put two and two together and figured out she was referring to one of our regular chapel attendees, who was very involved in the chapel ministry and a committed Christian. But this worker described her as "the lady who complains all the time." This woman had asked me many times to pray for a friend of hers, also at the center, who was not a follower of Christ. I visited this "non-believer" many times in the nursing home, and she was one of the happiest persons I have ever met. She was positive, thankful, and cheerful even though she was almost totally incapacitated. I admit that at times when I was a little low emotionally, I would arrange a visit with this lady because she would always pick up my spirits. Being a Christian will save a person, but it won't necessarily make them happy. Only having a good attitude will do that.

Being a Christian will save a person, but it won't necessarily make them happy. Only having a good attitude will do that.

I have seen people in the retirement center complaining about how unhappy they were the entire time they lived there. I would often get called in by staff to try to cheer up such individuals. Others were positive and happy, even though they had great physical and even mental limitations. I admit, I don't know how cheerful and happy I would be if I were confined to a hospital bed in a nursing home. Some of these people are extremely well adjusted and very happy. One lady in particular lost her husband and was forced to go from independent living to the health center (nursing home).

She had some physical and mental issues. She stood up in Chapel one Sunday and announced that her parents were doing great. Well, this lady is over 90 and her parents have been dead for decades. Yet every time I ask her how she is doing, she tells me she is wonderful. "The food is great, the help is great, and the activities are great." How do you like it here? "It's wonderful." I have told her many times, "Evelyn (not her real name), you are my hero" and she is. People like her are my heroes. I have seen many of them at the retirement center, and they are the kind of people I want to be like. Old age is really challenging. I can't tell you how many people have told me, "Chaplain, old age is not for sissies." It is true. I have witnessed the most devastating things that have happened to older people. But the people that adjust well in great adversity and have joy are my true heroes.

In the late 60s, there was a song by the rock group, The Who. It was called, "My Generation". One line in the song goes, "I hope I die before I get old." I can understand why some people feel this way after what I have witnessed. But my true heroes are those who face old age and its many adversities, or great debilitating trials at any age, with a smile. We want to have our financial houses in order, but to me that is not the most important thing.

B. Trust God

So many elderly people who have wisely saved and invested their money all their lives, find themselves on the brink of financial ruin as they face the high and escalating costs of assisted living and nursing home care. I have challenged many in our center to put their trust in God and not in their money. The truth is, nothing is for certain. The national unemployment rate was a healthy 3.6 percent in January of 2020. As of April, it rose to 14.7 percent. There were an estimated 22 million Americans out of work. Someone says, "I'm not worried about the economy, because I have my job." Millions of people, however, lost their "secure" jobs in just a matter of days. In 1933 the national unemployment rate was 25 percent, which is higher than it is today. But the number of people who were actually unemployed, 15 million, is much lower than it was at the height of the pandemic. If the corona virus is not contained, who knows how high our unemployment rate will actually soar?

Someone else may say, “Well, I rely on Social Security for my livelihood.” We’re told it will always be there for us, but who knows for sure? With fewer people working to support the Social Security coffers, and more people retiring and living longer than ever before, it may not be as secure as we think. The government has run up unimaginable debts and has added trillions of dollars to our national deficit just since the beginning of the year. Some financial analysts think that we don’t need to worry about our deficit because our debt-to-GDP ratio is a relatively low—108 percent compared, for example, to Japan’s 237 percent. Others ask how long we can keep borrowing money before lenders begin to question our ability to repay these huge loans.

Today, cash is king. Investors encourage having a lot of one’s portfolio in cash and fixed investments. (Not as many were saying that before the pandemic.) But even cash is not entirely secure. There may not be a run on the banks like there was in 1929 because of FDIC backing, but there is always the risk of inflation and hyperinflation that can occur during times of great economic distress. As the government prints more money to try to boost the economy, the value of the dollar becomes less and less. Germany suffered severe hyperinflation after World War II. I saw a picture of a woman in Germany, immediately after the war, pushing a wheel barrel of German Marks. The entire amount of cash would only purchase one loaf of bread.

Today, cash is king. Investors encourage having a lot of one’s portfolio in cash and fixed investments. But even cash is not entirely secure.

The stock market is not a safe and secure financial vehicle to depend on. It dropped almost a third of its value shortly after reaching its all-time highs in February of 2020. Although the markets have always eventually rebounded, even after huge drops, there are many people who have lost fortunes through investing in stocks and bonds.

Some people say that real estate is secure. But it too dropped in 2008. Houses went down in value, and many people were under water (owed more than what their homes were worth). Some say we should invest in art or precious metals. But I repeat, nothing is secure, and even if someone is well diversified (which is a good idea), if things get bad enough, there can be very little to hold onto. I never thought there would be shortages of paper products (toilet paper) and shortages of meat, but we saw it during the pandemic. I never would have imagined that the world's greatest superpower nation could be brought to its knees because of a virus. In 1918 yes but not today with our great medical knowledge and scientific resources. In 1918 the great flu, which killed 675,000 people in the U.S., eventually went away. Either it mutated into a less dangerous form, or it ran its course, or whatever. But some are saying that COVID-19 might always be with us in one form of another. It may return periodically with various levels of severity.

All of this is to say that we must put our trust in God. In spite of doing all the things that we have talked about, nothing is for certain. Even if there was no pandemic and everything was rosy financially, we never know what could happen. Someone could get cancer, or they could be seriously injured or killed in an auto accident. I had two good young friends, former parishioners, who died suddenly in farming accidents. Life is uncertain, so the bottom line is that our dependency must be on God. Don't put your trust in your money, because it might not be there tomorrow. The COVID-19 virus has shown that things suddenly can turn for the worse for everyone. Put your trust in God to take care of you.

"But blessed is the one who trusts in the Lord, whose confidence is in him. They will be like a tree planted by the water that sends out its roots by the stream. It does not fear when heat comes; its leaves are always green. It has no worries in a year of drought and never fails to bear fruit" (Jeremiah 17:7–8).

“Do not store up for yourselves treasures on earth, where moth and vermin destroy, and where thieves break in and steal. But store up for yourselves treasures in heaven, where moths and vermin do not destroy, and where thieves do not break in and steal. For where your treasure is, there your heart will be also.

“The eye is the lamp of the body. If your eyes are good, your whole body will be full of light. But if your eyes are unhealthy, your whole body will be full of darkness. If then the light within you is darkness, how great is that darkness!

“No one can serve two masters. Either you will hate the one and love the other, or you will be devoted to the one and despise the other. You cannot serve both God and money.

“Therefore I tell you, do not worry about your life, what you will eat or drink; or about your body, what you will wear. Is not life more than food, and the body more than clothes?
Look at the birds of the air; they do not sow or reap or store away in barns, and yet your heavenly Father feeds them. Are you not much more valuable than they? Can any one of you by worrying add a single hour to your life?

“And why do you worry about clothes? See how the lilies of the field grow. They do not labor or spin. Yet I tell you that not even Solomon in all his splendor was dressed like one of these.
If that is how God clothes the grass of the field, which is here today and tomorrow is thrown into the fire, will he not much more clothe you--you of little faith? So do not worry, saying, ‘What shall we eat?’ or ‘What shall we drink?’ or ‘What shall we wear?’

For the pagans run after all these things, and your heavenly Father knows that you need them. But seek first his kingdom and his righteousness, and all these things will be given to you as well. Therefore do not worry about tomorrow, for tomorrow will worry about itself. Each day has enough trouble of its own." (Matthew 6:19–34)

Chapter 14

A Word to the Big Guys

This book has been addressed to little guy and gals like me. It is addressed to the individuals who have not made a lot of money. I hope I have shown how by doing the right things and by living well, within your means, you can be quite comfortable when it the time to retire comes.

Now I want to say a word regarding the big guys, and there are many in our country. Some make more money than you and I could ever imagine. My wife and I visited my sister and her husband at their summer home one weekend. They took us out on a beautiful lake that was surrounded by gorgeous homes (mansions, from my perspective). My brother-in-law was calling out the names of famous wealthy people who owned them, usually as a summer residence. In that same area was the former summer home of a Christian financial advisor, whom I admired and had listened to often on the radio over the years. But this, again, is my point for writing this book. Financial advisors, worth millions of millions of dollars, who live lavish lifestyles that you and I can hardly imagine, are telling us how to manage our modest investments. It reminds me of pastor's conferences that I used to go to years ago. Usually, pastors of mega churches (churches of 25,000 people) would tell us little guys how to manage our churches of 80 to 100 people. They are really successful, and they make a lot of money through their books and TV programs, but somehow they just don't relate to me in my small world. This book is for the little guy from another little guy just like you who is handling his finances successfully. I am not writing to you from one of my many homes, hoping to make a killing on another bestselling book. I am just like you.

I do have just a word to say to say to the big guys who do make a lot of money. My question for you is, how much is enough? How much money do you really need to be happy? How many homes can you use at a time? How many cars? How many more financial projects do you need to take on so you can make more bundles of cash? I understand some of you have an incredible gift when it comes to finances. I have known people like you. A good friend from a former church told me, "Pastor, I don't have to work. I am 30 years old and I don't need to make any more money. I only work because I want to. My spiritual gift is that of making money." There may be many people like this. They have the Midas touch, and everything they handle seems to turn to gold. You big guys have a great responsibility, however. The Bible says that to whom much is given much is required (Luke 12:48). Giving 10 percent of your income is not enough. Even a little guy like me can do that. But you are a big guy, and you can do a lot more. So let me challenge you, instead of looking for more great deals and instead of getting more vacation homes, do this: Figure out the standard of living you want to live on. Keep your beautiful home or homes for all I care, your nice cars and toys, and vacations, but give the rest away. You may be able to live like a king on 20 percent and give the rest away. This is what my friend Don, whom I mentioned earlier, did and it is what some others do as well.

Joel Manby was an executive for Saturn Motors and later became CEO at an organization that ran theme parks like Dollywood. Like many CEOs, he made money hand over foot. But in his book *Love Works*, he told how for years he and his wife have done just what I am suggesting. He established a goal to have a certain net worth, and after he achieved it he gave the rest away.

You are not going to take it with you anyway, and sometimes adult children may do better with not inheriting so much. So, figure out what the good life is for you, and give the rest away. I am looking at my financial program right now, and at this point of the year my highest expense category is in what I have given away. Thirty-seven percent of my total spending is in giving. This is 20 percent more than my next expense category. But I'm just a little guy. You can do much better.

Chapter 15

Different Strokes for Different Folks and a Word of Compassion

I am just a little guy. I am the plodder, the tortoise on the slow and steady path who has done the right conservative things over many years, which has left me in good financial shape for retirement. But there are different ways of looking at finances. This has always been true, even within the Christian world. St. Francis of Assisi encouraged his followers to own as little as possible. He once chastised one of his monks for owning a coin. St. Francis led one of the many monastic orders in which it was seen as a sign of spirituality to beg for one's livelihood. I know Christian people today who give almost everything away. They don't beg for money, but when they get it they will soon find someone who needs it. I can't criticize them because they are following God's calling for their lives.

Then there are people who function well through managing loads of debt. I was pastor of a church in Minnesota made up of almost all farmers. They explained to me that in order to farm, a person has to go into debt. It is just the name of the game. Farmers would have to buy expensive equipment, not just so they could manage more acres, but so they could decrease their taxes. They always dealt in debt. Very few did not have to borrow to put in their crops. It was and is a whole different world to me. Friends told me that it was not unusual for them to write out checks exceeding $100,000. The slow and steady conservative approach that I have followed all my life just wouldn't work in their world. I realize this and I say, just keep doing what you're doing. Who am I to judge?

There are people who make a lot more money and they can do a lot more. They are in the fast lane. They have a lot and they spend a lot. Sometimes they're in debt but they can manage it well. They buy homes or cars that I wouldn't think of owning even if I had the money, because I just would never pay that much for a house or a car. But they do it, and it works well for them. I'm fine with it.

Then there are the big guys. They are risk takers, and they know how to make money and manage it. It would be silly for me to suggest that they do things on my simple tortoise-like pace. These people are movers and shakers in the financial world, and I am just not like them; I don't think like them. I'm too conservative. I say again, more power to them.

I have a friend who is a little guy like me. He doesn't have much but he has managed well, plodding along conservatively. He is doing well financially in terms of his retirement. His brother, on the other hand, is a big guy. His brother likes to take risks, and he has done extremely well. Years ago, my friend's brother told him that he was going to invest in a startup company that was opening a group of stores. He wanted my friend to invest 5 or 10 thousand in the company. Even though he had the money, he didn't want to do it. He was satisfied where he was. Sometime later, his brother asked him again, "Don't you want to invest in this great company? Just give me $5,000." My friend said, "No I don't think I want to do that." Well, the company was Wal-Mart, and my friend's brother made millions of dollars and now lives in a mansion in Arizona. My friend has regretted his decision, and who wouldn't, unless you can say, "Different strokes for different folks"? Some people are in the fast lane. They are oriented this way; more power to them. But most of us are not. It is OK to take the conservative approach and live well, within our means, and have a good retirement. We little guys aren't rich and are never going to be, but we can be happy and have more than enough to live comfortably.

We little guys aren't rich and are never going to be, but we can be happy and have more than enough to live comfortably.

Let's not forget the people who really struggle financially. Jesus said the "poor will always be with you." I want to emphasize that we do not need to condemn or judge those who are poor and needy. In former churches, I have witnessed some terrible hostility toward those who are poor. I have had to fight with the Board of Deacons just to give a single mom $50. Some people have a resentful attitude towards those who are struggling financially. They think the poor are in their financial situations because they don't want to work or because they have a welfare mentality. I'm not denying that some people have this mindset. But as I've explained to my former parishioners, poverty is more than not having enough money. It may be brought on by the way someone was raised. These ways of thinking have to be challenged if we really want to help people in need. We have to be compassionate about the way they live, understanding that if we had their backgrounds, we probably would be just like them. "But for the grace of God, there go I." I live in a poorer inner-city neighborhood, and I am constantly amazed by things I witness. For example, this morning I noticed that someone had thrown a container of soda out on my driveway. No problem, I just went out and picked it up. An hour later, I looked outside and I noticed four empty beer cans on my lawn. I can't tell you how often I've had to pick up garbage in my yard that has been thrown out of someone's car window (usually a rusty pick-up truck with no muffler). Neighbors just throw garbage out on their lawns and leave it there. I just wasn't raised this way, and it is difficult for me to understand. But this doesn't mean I should despise my neighbors or not try to help them. I was outside one day and I heard a neighbor cussing and swearing at his girlfriend's children who were staying with him for the weekend. I was appalled. How could anyone treat little children like that? One day I heard grown men screaming and yelling at each other outside a neighbor's house. The very same day the police were at another neighbor's house because of a woman fighting with her boyfriend. Another neighbor told me that one day he was sitting in his living room and bullets started coming through his house. I could go on and on, but what I'm saying is that we can despise and refuse to help people who do these kinds of things, or we can realize that poverty is a mindset that is greatly influenced by a person's background and environment. It is easy to write people off because we think they're not trying. But if we see the larger picture, we will believe we still need to help others, even if they do have a welfare mentality. I met so many Christians who were against helping the poor that I began to keep a record of scriptures that point out our responsibility to help those in need. I discovered that there are many references. The Lord did not say that we are to stop helping people if they don't clean up the trash in their yards or if they beat their girlfriends. We still have the responsibility. To whom much is given, much is required.

> "Then the King will say to those on his right, 'Come, you who are blessed by my Father; take your inheritance, the kingdom prepared for you since the creation of the world. For I was hungry and you gave me something to eat, I was thirsty and you gave me something to drink, I was a stranger and you invited me in. I needed clothes and you clothed me, I was sick and you looked after me, I was in prison and you came to visit me.'" (Matthew 25:34–36)

So, we need to be compassionate towards the poor and needy. They need our help, not our condemnation. A lot of churches give a large percentage of their incomes to missions, which is good, but many give very little to those who have financial need. This ought to change. If you are in a bad financial situation and are unemployed or underemployed, the Lord is your go-to person. I'm not saying you just need to sit in front of your TV and expect God to send someone to offer you a job. More often you are going to have to be diligent about finding work and/or improving your skills so you can find a job that will meet the needs of you and your family. Christian author and TV minister Andrew Womack encourages people in financial need t to not ask God to drop money in their lap, but to ask for his wisdom in how to make money.

Recently on a Christian TV program, a young couple told how they were on the brink of financial destruction. They had work but they didn't make enough to pay their bills. One night they stayed up all night praying for their terrible financial situation. During their prayer time, one of them saw a picture in their mind of a stick of honey and the other saw a mental picture of a honey jar. They were shocked when they heard that each had envisioned a very similar thing. To make a long story short, they went into beekeeping, which at first supplemented their income but eventually blossomed into a new business that tripled what they were previously making. If you are poor, I would encourage you to seek God's help and his wisdom on how to proceed. He might lead you to get more education or further training so you can get a better paying job. We need to have tolerance and compassion for one another. There are certainly different strokes for different folks when it comes to money.

Chapter 16

Encouragement for those with No Retirement Savings

A 57 year old woman expressed how she wanted to retire in seven years but had absolutely nothing in retirement savings. She said she made $80,000 a year in her job as a nurse manager and had $3600 in monthly expenses which included a $1600 monthly mortgage and a $400 monthly car payment. She also reported $5000 in credit card debt. The woman wrote into a retirement advisor and wanted to know if there was any way she could possibly make retirement work for her someday. (Malito, Alessandra "Help Me Retire" MarketWatch, Dec 6, 2020, 11:04 a.m. ET)

Here's how I would have responded to the woman and to the many persons who are nearing retirement age with little or no savings. First, I would encourage those in this situation to not condemn themselves for the situation that that they are faced with. None of us can change our past. The past is what it is. Beating yourself up over what you should have done differently may keep you from making needed changes. Understand that there is hope for you to retire even if there is a goose egg in your savings account. Here's the deal: Instead of beating yourself up over what you did wrong, start doing things right now. You might not be able to build up a huge retirement nest egg, but even a small one is better than no nest egg at all. The key is to decide that you are going to make changes to your financial situation that will positively affect your ability to retire. If you want to do things the same way you always have, you will find yourself in the same situation you are in now five years down the line. "I'm not going to beat myself up over what I did wrong, but I'm going to start doing things right, so I can retire." The minister in me would encourage you to ask for and accept God's forgiveness for past mistakes and to ask for his help in making needed changes. "If we confess our sins, he is faithful and just to forgive us our sins and to cleanse us of all unrighteousness." I John 1:9 "Commit to the LORD whatever you do, and your plans will succeed." Proverbs 16:3. It is going to be difficult to correct old patterns that have been established for years, but with God's help you can do it and be able to have a workable retirement.

So let's consider the woman's example mentioned above. I would tell her to be willing to make sacrifices over the next several years so she can reach her retirement goals. The first thing that I noticed is that her mortgage is $1600 a month. That seems awfully high although I understand the cost of housing is outrageous in some parts of the country. I would do something to decrease my housing costs. Find a less expensive home or a cheaper rental. Or consider having a roommate for a few years that will help with the expenses. Say a roommate could pay $800 a month. That would help significantly. One of the killers for retirees is the cost of housing. We have to find ways to minimize it. Failing to do so can harm one's ability to have a good retirement or even jeopardize it entirely. "But I don't want to have a roommate; I like having my own place." Remember we're talking sacrifice. That's the only way we can build a small nest egg significant enough to allow us to retire when we're starting our savings plan very late.

The minister in me needs to say something else right here on the subject of roommates. I'm not talking about "living with someone" and having sexual relationships with them. You can't expect God to help you salvage your financial situation if you are living disobediently to him. Make sure if you have a roommate everything is on the up and up.

The second thing that I noticed about the woman's financial situation was her car payment of $400 a month. I would get rid of the car and drive something that I could pay cash for. If it is only a $2000 car, so be it. The last thing the woman needs is a car payment. In fact it is the last thing anyone needs who is trying to prepare for retirement. "But I can't do that. I can't give up my new car. How would I get to work? I can't be driving an old piece of unreliable junk." Remember the key word is "sacrifice". We are going to do difficult things, do without, and make necessary sacrifices so we can retire. Understand that we will have to endure these hardships only for a short while, so that we can someday enjoy our retirement years.

Then of course the credit card debt also needs to be addressed. I would tell the woman she would not only need to pay off that debt as quickly as possible, but she would have to determine to never go in debt again. This is a new way of thinking for a lot of people today. The old way was when we wanted something we would simply go ahead and charge it. The new way is to establish a workable budget and determine to never buy anything on credit. Never charge anything. If you can't pay cash for it you shouldn't be even considering it. The only thing you should ever make payments on is your mortgage and you want to get that paid off as soon as possible. Get rid of all your debts, live within your budget, and only pay cash for stuff.

I would also tell the woman to start contribute to her retirement savings as soon as possible. Go to your employer and get your retirement contributions set up as soon as possible. If your employer is willing to match your contributions in a 401(K) have them do it. You want to contribute as much as you possibly can to your retirement savings while you are still able to work. Who knows maybe in seven years time you can build up a nest egg of 200 to 250 thousand dollars. This is not huge amount in terms of a retirement savings, but remember a small nest egg is better than none at all.

At age 57 I would invest the funds in my 401(K) aggressively. In other words I would put them in high yielding mutual funds. If the market crashes you will still have seven or so years to recover. Because you are building up a nest egg from ground zero, you are going to have to take some investment risks. Investing in something that pays 1% interest is not going to do the trick. Then as you get older and closer to your retirement years you invest more conservatively meaning you put more in bonds and fixed income sources.

In 2008 the housing market crashed and the great recession ruined the retirement dreams of many would be retirees. Many had to delay their retirement for several years. I was about 55 years of age at the time and my retirement savings took a significant hit because I was invested very aggressively. I wasn't worried however because I knew that I had ten to twelve years for the markets to recover. Many during this time took their retirement savings out of the financial markets and put them in safe C/D's and government bonds. Afterwards and throughout the coming years the markets not only recovered their losses but made tremendous gains. Those who stayed in the market did very well but those who removed their money during the recession faced great losses. Remember the trick is to buy when the markets are low and to sell when they are high. It is amazing how many people do just the opposite often because they panic when things start to go south. Many also buy stocks when the markets are high. This is not the way to do it.

I enjoyed tremendous market gains through riding out the recession. My total retirement portfolio gained hundreds of thousands of dollars during this period. But as I got closer to my retirement years I invested less aggressively and put more into bonds and fixed securities. If you are 57 with nothing saved for retirement, I would be aggressive for several years and then gradually shift to more conservative investments.

As everybody knows, when you retire you can begin to collect Social Security. Actually you can collect before you retire at the age of 62 but it isn't highly recommended. Almost all financial advisors suggest waiting until age 70 before collecting. But if you are 57 with nothing saved for retirement, it is strongly advisable to wait until age 70. There are two reasons for this: First, you earn 8% more from Social Security for each year you wait beyond age 62. Second, since you won't have a large nest egg to draw on because you started your retirement savings late, you will need the highest amount you possibly can from your Social Security. Someone who retires at 66 or 67, which is full retirement age for most recent retirees, can start taking Social Security earlier if they have a million and a half stored up. But if they only have $200,000 in retirement savings, they are going to really need to maximize their Social Security payments in order to make ends meet.

If you have little or no retirement savings, you are probably going to have to work longer than the traditional 65 or 66 years of age. That is OK. There are a lot of good things about continuing to work. Work keeps you active, and socially engaged. It gives you purpose and something to get up for in the morning. Many people think work is a curse but did you know that work existed before the fall of mankind? In the book of Genesis, God did not give work to Adam and Eve because they had sinned. They actually were given work before they ate the forbidden fruit. They took care of the Garden of Eden and Adam named the animals. All of this is to say that work is a blessing and not a curse. It is OK to keep working beyond full retirement age and to even work part time for many years to come should health permit. If you haven't saved much for your retirement, one of the things you can do is to work longer. Some people have the financial means to retire but choose to continue to work way beyond their full retirement age. In my city there is a judge who continues to serve behind the bench even though she is over 90 years old. I love it. My sister is 71 and she is CEO of an organization and she has no plans to retire. Her husband is 72 and he is employed and s I mentioned is changing jobs because he wants a new challenge. The word "retirement" isn't even in his grid. "Why would I ever want to retire? I love what I'm doing." As the old saying goes, "Fall in love with your job and you'll never work another day in your life." Perhaps when you reach your desired retirement age you can try another career, something different than what you've done the last 40 years. I thought of that myself. My ideal job would be to drive cars for automobile dealers. "Drive this car to St. Louis and pick up another at so and so dealership and drive it back here." That sounds like a fun retirement job to me. Unfortunately, because of my wife's health I was unable to consider it. But there may be some fun retirement job you can do for a change of pace that will give you more of a desire to keep working. I have a friend that retired from his construction business after many years and became a greeter at Wal-Mart. You talk about someone who was made for a job. My friend is friendly and outgoing and he absolutely loved it. You might not see yourself as a greeter at Wal-Mart but there might be some fund retirement job that you would love.

You might not be able to retire where you are presently living because the cost of living is too high. But you might be able to pull it off if you move to a less expensive area. If you have little or no retirement savings, this is something that could help your financial situation immensely. As I mentioned before, it is not always advisable to move from family and friends. Some who do end up moving back "home" after a few troublesome months or years. But making such a move might be necessary for those who have started to save for their retirement late in life.

An essential part of salvaging one's retirement due to a lack of savings is cost cutting. Figure out how much you spend every year and on what. Then create a budget while reducing or eliminating all unnecessary expenses. You might be used to eating out four times a week and taking expensive vacations. These things you are going to have to cut out while you are scrambling for these next years. Remember it is all about sacrificing for a few years so you will be able to retire in a few years to come. Cut out the fat. Reduce your spending and increase what you save. Cut the cable, get rid of the second car, do whatever it takes so you will at least have something to supplement your Social Security. Working extra hours or taking on a part time job on top of your regular one is also a possibility. Remember it is only for a few short years. If you can drastically cut your expenses and greatly increase what you save you may even be able to build a nest egg of $250,000 or more. That's not a million but it is significant. You could take that money and put some of it into an annuity and/or high paying dividend stocks. This monthly income will help to supplement your Social Security. When you retire, you might need a part time job for a while but you can reach your retirement goals if you are willing to discipline yourself now.

Summary: If you are near retirement age and you haven't saved a nickel, all is not lost. There is hope for you. But you will have to change the way you have done things in the past. You will have to cut your expenses, and save like you never have before. You will have to sacrifice for a few years, so you can someday be able to retire. It can happen and it will happen with God's help. Be encouraged. Yes you can retire.

Chapter 17

Conclusion

This book is written to the little guy, people like me who have never made a lot of money. I have shown you how I, by living conservatively but well, have been able to enter retirement reasonably financially secure. There are others who have made a lot more money than I have but have not been able to retire because they have overspent, invested unwisely, or failed to save for retirement. I am the tortoise and they are the hare. Although they have been in the fast lane and I have been in the slow lane, I have made it to the finish line before them. I have done this by living within my budget, saving, giving, and most of all, by putting my trust in God. You might think that none of this is new and that there is nothing profound about what I am saying. I would agree. There is nothing new about what I am saying, but the truth is, most people aren't doing it.

Maybe you've heard the story of the preacher who preached the same sermon every Sunday. At first it was really good. People were enjoying it and getting motivated. But after a while, people started to complain. One gentleman finally got up the nerve to ask him, "How come you preach the same old thing week after week? When are you going to start preaching something new?"

The preacher looked at him said, "I'll start preaching something new when you and everyone else around here actually start doing what I've been telling you to do week after week." I'm preaching the same old sermon that financial advisors have been preaching week after week. I'm preaching it because many people still aren't getting it. There are more sermons to come that others will preach, but we have to start putting this one into practice before we'll be ready to hear the next ones. I wish you success, my fellow little guy, as you endeavor to live well, within your means. May you enter into your retirement "sitting pretty".

Epilogue: After much stress of living in a noisy high crime neighborhood, I and my wife moved temporarily into the retirement center where I served as a chaplain for 10 years. Then we purchased a small retirement style ranch home just a few blocks from where the retirement center is located. I had to pay Neighborhood Finance Corporation $7100 because I didn't stay the five years as agreed upon. I also gave up the remainder of our ten year tax abatement and a brand new house with new appliances etc. But it was well worth it. I don't regret selling the house at all. The incident shows that there is a lot more to consider besides money when it comes to retirement. It also shows that there are always lessons to be learned no matter how old we are.

Craig & Mary's Retirement Home

Craig Richard Burton is a graduate of College of DuPage in Glen Ellen, Illinois, North Central College in Naperville, Illinois and of Northern Baptist Theological Seminary (Now Northern Seminary), in Lombard, Illinois, where he earned his Masters of Christian Education and Masters of Divinity degrees. He has been a pastor in Illinois, Minnesota, and Iowa. He served at the Evangelical Free Church of Keokuk, Iowa for 18 years. For the last 10 years, he served as chaplain at Valley View Village Retirement Center. He retired in March of 2020. He and his wife, Mary, make their home in Des Moines, Iowa. They have two adult children, Eric and Rhett. Craig's hobbies are running, swimming, bicycling, reading, and writing. He still enjoys visiting with the elderly.

………………………………END…………………………..

www.ingramcontent.com/pod-product-compliance
Ingram Content Group UK Ltd.
Pitfield, Milton Keynes, MK11 3LW, UK
UKHW021909190726
13853UKWH00002B/591

9 798527 964677